A Mom's Guide to Raising Thriving Kids with ADHD

The 8 Power Traits Every Parent Needs to Turn Struggle into Strength

Angel McKim

Happy Revolutions Media

For Scott, Ryan, and Colin—

You are my heart, my reason, and my greatest adventure.

Thank you for the warm hugs, the back patio talks, and the spontaneous sprints through the house—both of us laughing like I might still catch you.

This book exists because of you. And for you.

Contents

Part 1: The Power Traits Approach to Parenting a Child with ADHD

Every thriving family starts with a parent who's learning right alongside their child.

CHAPTER 1

The Wake-Up Call

I didn't know it yet, but that day marked the beginning of a revolution—not just in how I parented, but in who I was becoming.

We were excited about the new school year. We had just moved into a new house, a new state, and the excitement of change was energizing. But going to school was when everything changed.

I stood outside my son's classroom in the cold, echoey hallway of the elementary school, waiting for my 3:30 appointment with his 5th-grade teacher, Mrs. G.

My body was tense with anticipation as I stood with my husband, silently staring at the classroom door decorated with pictures of happy, smiling students. After what felt like an eternity, my son's teacher opened the door, turned on a strained smile, and gestured for us to come in.

We sat together at the "instruction table," delicately perched on two plastic kid-sized chairs, his teacher sitting directly across from us. I couldn't shake the awkward feeling that I was now a student in her class, about to be shamed for all the things I just couldn't seem to fix.

After all, this wasn't the first time I had spoken with her. Just a few weeks into the school year, her tidy, perfectly aligned notes showed up in my son's school planner:

"Your son was disrupting my lesson today and had to sit in the hall."

"Today he could not finish his work—he was just staring off into space."

"He missed recess again today because he couldn't finish his classwork."

So when his teacher slid a stack of graded papers across the table and stopped abruptly in front of me, I braced myself. It was more of the same.

"D+ Messy handwriting. I can't read this."

"C- You can do better than this!"

And it was followed by an oversized stack of more examples of his unfinished, messy work.

As I thumbed through the loose papers and wrinkled tests, Mrs. G sat with her hands neatly folded and took a breath as she prepared to tell me all the ways my son was struggling in class. I felt her judgment sear my skin as she began to speak.

"He can't sit still." "He's noisy and disruptive to his classmates." "None of the other students want to work with him because he doesn't do his share of the work."

I shifted uncomfortably in my tiny chair, attempting to hold back the wave of tears about to erupt from my eyes.

I wanted to tell her he was trying. That I was trying. But the words stayed stuck in my throat.

Mrs. G continued—listing all the strategies she'd collected over her 16-year career to help students like my son.

"I put him in the back of the room, then tried moving him to the front of the class. It simply doesn't matter where he sits. I am constantly prompting and tapping him on the shoulder to remind him to start again on his work. I write all assignments on the whiteboard with each step outlined in great detail."

"OK," I said. "I get it. What can I do? What do you want me to do?"

Mrs. G paused, looked down at her folded hands, and began to tell me a story about her own son. How he too had struggled in school. How she helped him. And how he persevered and is now thriving as a middle schooler.

As she handed me a box of tissues, I wiped my eyes and asked the obvious next question.

"What did you do?"

Mrs. G started again.

"Well, I've been teaching for 16 years, and I've seen this before. If I were you, I would have him tested for ADHD. It's more common than you think."

"For what?" I asked.

"Attention Deficit Hyperactivity Disorder," she explained.

My hands were fidgety as I stared at my wrinkled, snotty tissue. My mind was racing—full of confusion, fear, and perhaps even a little excitement. Because maybe, if it worked for her son, it could also work for mine.

She scribbled a phone number on my son's conference summary, and we left.

Becoming the Researcher, Advocate, and Exhausted Mom

The very next day, I scheduled an intake appointment with the neuropsychologist Mrs. G had recommended and began researching ADHD like my life depended on it. I learned about helpful supplements like omega-3s, trace minerals, and the importance of nutrition, exercise, and—of course—sleep.

"Check," I said out loud, mentally ticking each one off my list. I was doing it all. I was ambitious and deeply committed to figuring out how to help my son and get him back on track. After all, I'm a nurse—I know how to navigate the healthcare system. "I got this," I told myself.

I clung to that thought like a life raft—even when the waters got rougher by the week.

But as those weeks turned into months, frustration crept in. I was doing everything everyone told me to do. Sleep? Check. Nutrition? Check. Exercise? Check. Parent behavior training? Check. Supplements? Check.

We had tried everything—except one thing. Medication.

And if you've ever considered ADHD meds for your child, then you've probably asked the same questions I did:

How do they work?

How long will he have to take them?

What are the risks?

Will insurance cover them?

Are there long-term effects if he takes them for years?

I didn't want to put my child on medication. Honestly, I had zero desire to go down that path. But my desperation to help him was louder than my fear.

The Text That Should Have Felt Like a Win

Weeks later—and after several full-blown arguments with my husband—I found myself sitting in the pediatrician's office, holding a prescription for Quillivant XR, a popular extended-release stimulant used to treat kids with ADHD.

He started the medication the very next morning. I sent a note to his teacher so she could keep an eye on him at school. Later that day, to my surprise, Mrs. G sent me a "love note." It was a text with a photo of my son sitting calmly at his desk, complete with a smile emoji and a little red heart.

"What a difference! My classroom is so quiet!" And it was true. He could sit. He could focus. He could finish his work. But as I read her text, I didn't feel elated. I didn't feel relieved. I felt... off.

Inside me, emotions tumbled like a load of laundry in the dryer—relief tangled with sadness, hope knotted up with confusion. A little peace mixed with a whole lot of unease.

"So this is it?" I asked myself. "Is this what it takes for him to succeed? For him to be happy?"

I felt conflicted. Years—or even a lifetime—of medication, appointments, dosage tweaks, and pharmacy pickups wasn't the picture I had in mind when I dreamed of helping my son thrive.

Something still felt missing. But I couldn't put my finger on what.

> "Sometimes the questions are complicated and the answers are simple." – Dr. Seuss

I began to ask myself more questions.

"What skills does my son actually need to feel happy and fulfilled in his life?"

"What will help him persevere through whatever challenges come his way—especially knowing he might face more than most?"

"What does he need to be successful—not just academically, but as a human being?"

Those questions took me down a completely different rabbit hole. Not toward more charts, meds, or management plans—but toward something deeper.

I started reading about the science of happiness, the habits of mental fitness, the research on well-being, and most importantly, the real-life stories of moms who had already raised thriving adults with ADHD.

"Yes! Yes!" I blurted out loud one night while reading. Yes—this is what he needs. These are the skills I want to teach him. These are the things that matter most.

Things like resilience, motivation, problem-solving, and grit. Confidence. Empathy. Emotional regulation. Decision-making. Joy.

It's Not Just About the Diagnosis

This wasn't just about grades or behavior anymore. This was about real-life tools—skills that could help him thrive not just in school, but for life.

And that's exactly what I want to share with you: The power traits—those core, must-have skills that moms before us have used to guide their kids through hard seasons and into adulthood with strength and self-worth. Along the way, I'll share the best tools and strategies I've gathered—not just as a nurse or a life coach—but as a mom who's been right where you are.

Our kids are constantly growing and changing—moment to moment, situation to situation. But what doesn't change? The foundation.

What This Book Is Really About

That's what this book is about. The lasting, transferable skills your child can carry into every season of life. The tools you can use to build stronger relationships, a more peaceful home, and a future you actually feel excited about.

This journey of parenting a child with ADHD isn't always easy. But if you're ready to grow—not just as a parent, but as a person—then this can be one of the most meaningful, life-changing journeys you'll ever take.

This book is here to be your map. Your toolbox. Your pep talk. And maybe even your new best friend.

Because while there's no one right way to raise a child with ADHD, there are powerful, proven ingredients that can make your unique parenting recipe a whole lot more nourishing—for both of you.

Flip through almost any parenting book today, and you'll see the same familiar pillars: warmth, attachment, boundaries, and autonomy.

Experts and researchers often use these pillars to define the three classic parenting styles: permissive, punitive, and authoritative.

On one end of the spectrum: permissive parenting: It's warm, loving, and emotionally open—but often missing structure, consistency, and follow-through.

Research suggests permissive parenting is too soft to be effective long-term.

On the opposite end, you'll find punitive parenting—strict, rigid, and rooted in control. The goal here is obedience, not connection. And while it might get short-term compliance, research shows it's too harsh to build lasting growth.

And just like in the story of Goldilocks, there's a "just right" option we're encouraged to aim for: authoritative parenting.

Authoritative parents balance warmth and boundaries. They're sensitive to their child's needs, but they also hold firm limits and encourage independence.

Sounds great, right?

Here's what I remember instead:

It was a Tuesday night, and my 11-year-old was sitting at the kitchen table, slumped over a half-finished worksheet. I could tell he was trying—not just with the writing, but to hold it together. His pencil tapped the page in this slow, heavy rhythm, and then he quietly whispered, "I'm just not good at this stuff."

And something about the way he said it—so soft, so certain—made my chest ache.

At that moment, I didn't care what parenting style I was supposed to be following. I just wanted to scoop him up, erase the shame, and remind him that he is so much more than a worksheet.

And that's the tension so many of us live in—between what experts tell us should work and what it actually feels like when your child is falling apart in front of you.

Because even the best ADHD tools feel useless when you're standing in the school parking lot, holding back tears after another rough drop-off—or trying to navigate a homework battle for the fourth night in a row.

So many of those "proven strategies" sound great on paper. They come with neat steps, official terms, and expert backing. But in real life? We forget them the second your child melts down over the wrong spoon or refuses to put on socks.

And honestly? Parenting isn't about memorizing a set of tactics or getting every moment right.

It's about showing up in the mess. It's about knowing your child, trusting yourself, and learning how to stay steady when everything around you feels like chaos.

That's why I've chosen a simpler path—one built for real-life parenting, not picture-perfect ideals.

You don't need more research to study or a script to follow. You need something real. Something practical. Something you can actually reach for when things get hard—because they will.

Let's Begin This Together

This isn't a textbook. And it's definitely not a clinical manual.

While it's rooted in strong science, this book offers something different—something built on warmth, wisdom, and the messy beauty of real life.

It's a new way of thinking about parenting—based on warmth, wisdom, and real-world application. You'll hear from moms who've walked this road—moms who made it through the hard seasons and came out stronger.

You'll try out tools that strengthen your own mental fitness muscles, and help your child do the same. But more than anything, I hope this book helps you pause and ask better questions. The kind that lead you to look again—at your child, your home, and even yourself—with clearer eyes and a more hopeful heart.

I'm still on this ADHD parenting journey, too. And I've been deeply inspired by the moms who came before us—those who weathered the storms and found a way through.

There's a better way to help our kids. A better way to help them thrive—without losing yourself in the process. And I'm honored to share it with you.

CHAPTER 2

The 8 Power Traits of an ADHD-Savvy Mom

I didn't get here overnight—and I don't expect you to either. But I'll tell you what I wish someone had told me sooner: there's a better way to raise a child with ADHD. And it starts here.

Sometimes we stumble into the work that changes everything. Sometimes our calling finds us. I certainly didn't expect to be handed mine with my son's ADHD diagnosis.

In October 2019, I launched my coaching business to support the chaotic lives of working moms—the same year my son was diagnosed with ADHD.

As I shifted my focus to learning everything I could about ADHD, my business pivoted, too. Soon I began supporting the rollercoaster lives of moms of kids with ADHD.

I started writing weekly emails about my own experiences and, like everyone else in the ADHD space, I focused on behavior management, homework strategies, scaffolding weaknesses, school accommodations, social skills, and college preparation.

And I did learn a lot. But as I connected with more and more moms, I began to see that the ADHD parenting roller coaster wasn't your average ride.

It felt more like one of those old wooden roller coasters—jerky, unpredictable, and relentless. Raising a child with ADHD is no joke.

In fact, the more I learned about ADHD, the more my optimism for my son's future began to waver. And if you're anything like me, you've read all the same terrifying statistics.

Kids with ADHD are more likely to have accidents, get into car crashes, and struggle with behavior at school. They're at greater risk for addiction, anxiety, and depression.

The medical community is quick to point out the risks—but slow to offer hope.

And when the weight of all that fear pressed in, I found myself giving a pep talk to the only person I could control: me.

"Okay, Angel. What part of you can help the most right now?"

The project manager part of me stepped forward and began going through my mental checklist. Again.

By that point, I had taken on so many new roles: the tutor, the homework checker, the appointment maker, the supplement selector... and the shrewd critic of everything my son wasn't doing.

And still—I wondered if I was doing enough. If I was enough.

But if I'm being honest, I didn't just want to help—I wanted to be the hero. I wanted to swoop in and fix it all. To be the one who made it all better.

And in spite of all the effort—the diet changes, the supplements, the structured routines—it still wasn't enough. I didn't feel victorious. I didn't feel proud. I felt... uninspired. And at times, life just felt hard.

And if you've ever found yourself here too—tired, disheartened, wondering if your doing the right things—you're not failing.

You're walking the hard, hidden road that real growth asks of us.

As I coached more moms, I realized I wasn't alone.

We were all tired—not just from the ADHD parenting itself, but from trying so hard to manage symptoms and shape our kids into model students.

And that's when I began to see the bigger issue.

Sure, these kids—ADHD, dyslexia, anxiety, you name it—were learning something. (But not the skills they actually needed most.)

Everything was focused on controlling behavior, boosting academics, and meeting expectations. But no one was teaching the essential life skills of resilience, emotional regulation, well-being, and mental fitness.

It might look like thriving when a child gets good grades and follows the rules.

But really?

We were teaching them how to survive.

Survive school.

Survive social situations.

Survive their own wiring.

And it hit me hard: Nothing about that felt inspiring.

So I started asking myself new questions:

"If his life feels hard and uninspired now—as a successful student—how will adulthood feel any different?" "If he's struggling to feel joy as a child, what will magically change when he's older?"

Sure, he was succeeding on paper. But inside? He wasn't lit up. He wasn't thriving.

He was following the rules, taking the meds, doing the work... but his struggle followed him everywhere, like a shadow he couldn't shake...

Beyond Surviving

For some moms of kids with ADHD, a shiny report card is enough. If the report card makes it to the fridge and the honor roll photo gets posted on Facebook, that's good enough. But not for me. I wanted more.

My son deserves more than just surviving. All kids with ADHD deserve more. They deserve to live inspired, meaningful lives—lives filled with purpose and possibility.

That's when something shifted. I stopped chasing perfection and started chasing purpose. My new mission was clear: understand what truly helps kids with ADHD grow up to thrive.

I started obsessively researching the childhoods of successful adults with ADHD. Olympic gold medalist Michael Phelps. Billionaire entrepreneur Richard Branson. Award-winning author Dav Pilkey just to name a few.

I wanted to know what their moms did. What helped them thrive? What did their parents do differently? How did they raise kids who defied the statistics?

I dove in. I journaled, studied, and followed every rabbit hole. I kept asking myself: "What can I learn from these moms who've already done it? What if I used their success stories to examine my own parenting? What if their wins could shine a light on my strengths—and my blind spots?"

And slowly, a pattern began to emerge. Certain themes showed up again and again—key ingredients that every successful mom seemed to use.

These were the high-quality ingredients I'd been searching for. Not just tips and tricks. Not just behavior strategies. But real, powerful traits that made a difference.

Did these moms master every skill? No. But each one was really good at at least a few of them. And the best part? These skills already exist inside all of us—to varying degrees.

Each of these 'supermoms' had a unique strength—and that strength became exactly what their child needed most. These weren't just scaffolds or surface-level strategies. They were deep-rooted mental fitness skills that helped their families thrive.

"If there's a recipe for raising a thriving child with ADHD, it starts with choosing the right ingredients—ones that don't just manage behavior, but nurture growth, resilience, and joy." – Angel McKim

The Ingredients That Matter Most

You don't have to start from scratch—you just need to get intentional. These aren't abstract concepts or personality types. They're what I call Power Traits—and they're the heart of this book.

You don't need to be a perfect parent to raise a happy, successful child with ADHD. (Thank goodness, right?) What you do need is heart, intention, and a few key traits that can change everything.

Power Traits aren't about having it all figured out. They're about how you show up—especially when things are messy, unpredictable, or completely upside-down. They shape your child's self-worth, your connection with them, and their ability to thrive in a world that doesn't always work the way their brain does.

Some of the stories ahead will touch your heart. Some will make you laugh out loud. And all of them will remind you: growth is messy, brave, and worth it.

Introducing the Power Traits:

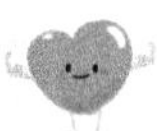

Unshakable Love & Acceptance

- My child knows they are loved no matter what

- I separate their behavior from their worth

- I make home feel like a safe, soft landing

Curiosity Instead of Judgment

- I ask "What's going on here?" instead of "Why did you do that?!"

- I try to understand the why behind the behavior

- I remind myself that all behavior is communication

Consistency with Flexibility

- I aim for rhythms, not rigid rules

- I hold boundaries with warmth

- I adjust when life throws us curveballs—without shame

Problem-Solving Over Punishment

- When something goes wrong, I partner with my child to find solutions

- I focus on teaching, not just consequences

- I remind myself that growth is the goal, not perfection

Strength-Based Focus

- I notice what lights my child up

- I praise effort, creativity, and unique strengths

- I help them feel seen for who they are, not just what they do

Staying Steady—Even When They're Not

- I notice when I'm dysregulated and take space when needed

- I use calming tools and talk openly about big feelings

- I model how to repair after a rough moment

Advocacy & Willingness to Learn

- I research, ask questions, and push back when needed

- I don't wait for permission to do what's best for my child

- I remind myself I am the expert on my kid

Playfulness & Humor

- I bring lightness to hard moments when I can

- I make space for joy and silliness, even when things feel heavy

- I use laughter as connection, not just a distraction

You don't need to master all of them at once. But as you read, I invite you to reflect on your strengths—and your stretch zones. Each mom in the coming chapters embodies one or more of these traits in a unique and powerful way.

Now, let's see what this looks like in real life. The moms you're about to meet aren't perfect. They're human. They're brave. They're powerful. And so are you.

"You're already doing the hardest part: showing up." –
Angel McKim

Part 2: Real Moms, Real Power Traits

The goal isn't to control the moment—it's to shape the direction.

CHAPTER 3

Strengths, Structure and the Long Game—Debbie's Story

Where my story met fear, Debbie's met fierce belief—and shows us how structure and strengths can shift the entire game.

Moms wear so many hats. But perhaps the most powerful one we ever step into is that of a team coach—the head coach of our own family.

That's exactly how Debbie Phelps approached raising her son, Michael Phelps—the most decorated U.S. Olympic athlete in history. Long before Michael Phelps became a household name, Debbie simply called her family "Team Phelps."

In those early years, Debbie was a home economics teacher, and her husband Fred was a state trooper. They lived in a typical middle-class neighborhood near Baltimore, Maryland, where Michael attended public school. When Michael was seven, his parents divorced. In her memoir *Debbie Phelps: A Mother for All Seasons*, she shares the story of parenting Michael through those formative years.

Like many kids with ADHD, Michael began to struggle in grade school. By third grade, Debbie was frequently hearing the same kinds of comments from teachers:

- "Michael has a hard time sitting still."

- "Michael doesn't show much interest in reading."

- "His inability to focus is disruptive to the classroom... there may be difficulties ahead."

If you're raising a child with ADHD, you might recognize the pattern:

- Struggles in school — with academics, behavior, or both.

- Teacher concerns — shared often, and usually focused on deficits.

- Professional support sought — often centering around behavior management, medication, and scaffolding.

- Accommodations implemented — to reduce symptoms and manage behavior.

And for many kids, that's where the story ends. But Debbie chose another path.

She didn't blindly accept the limitations others placed on her son. She listened—but she also trusted what she knew deep down. When teachers underestimated Michael's potential, Debbie didn't argue or explain. She simply and confidently said:

"You're wrong."

When teachers insisted Michael couldn't focus, she pointed them toward what they hadn't seen:

"You haven't watched him sit at a swim meet for four hours, waiting for his turn to compete. Don't tell me he can't focus—he can. When learning is meaningful and authentic, a child will sit forever."

It would have been easy for Debbie to shrink under the weight of all those criticisms. But instead, she stood tall—gathering every glimpse of focus, passion, and brilliance only she had seen—and said, with quiet certainty: "You're wrong about my child."

Imagine that for a second. Imagine hearing all the ways your child is "less than"—and instead of shrinking, you choose to stand tall.

Maybe, like Debbie, you've already had those moments too—the ones where you spoke up, even when your voice shook. The ones where you didn't just see a diagnosis—you saw your child's brilliance, waiting to be noticed. **That matters more than you know.**

Debbie didn't deny Michael's challenges. But she refused to let them define him. She was constantly on the lookout for sparks of curiosity and drive—and she used those passions as bridges to growth.

One of the ways she put that belief into practice? She met him exactly where his passions already lived. When it came to school-work, Debbie and Michael found a strategy that clicked:

"With subjects like English composition, we found that the best way for him to understand abstract problems was to convert them into real-world examples. If a math problem could be framed in terms of swim times or pools, he could practically do calculus in his head. When he had the freedom to use his rich visual imagination to create stories, he could structure them beautifully—just like a race, with a beginning, middle, and end."

This is strength-based parenting in action—one of the core power traits that sets successful ADHD parents apart. Debbie didn't just manage symptoms. She leaned into what Michael could do. She believed in him. She got creative. She coached from his strengths—not his shortcomings.

Her "Team Coach" mindset shows us what's possible when we stop trying to "fix" our kids—and start building their capacity instead. And that's something every ADHD parent can practice.

We don't have to be perfect. But we do have to believe—in our kids, in their potential, and in ourselves. And part of believing in what's possible for our kids means knowing we can't do it alone.

The Team Behind Every Triumph

Debbie knew she couldn't do it all alone. Fortunately, neither could Bob Bowman—Michael's swim coach and one of her most important partners along the way.

In his book *The Golden Rules*, Bob describes how "Team Phelps" extended far beyond just himself, Debbie, and Michael. It became a full circle of personal coaches—friends, family, teachers, and mentors—who inspired, guided, and encouraged Michael at every stage.

This idea—of intentionally building a team—is one of Bob's core principles:

> *"To successfully reach your vision, you will need supporters—friends, family members, coaches, bosses, co-workers, colleagues, and teachers—who believe in you." – Bob Bowman*

Michael's circle was bigger than most people realized. It wasn't just his coach and his mom. His older sisters, Hilary and Whitney, were there too—traveling the world to cheer him on from the stands.

There was Cathy Bennett, his first swim teacher, who helped him conquer his fear of putting his face in the water. There were doctors, trainers, and sports psychologists—each stepping in at different stages of his journey.

Bob recognized something many parents eventually come to understand—often the hard way: True success—especially when raising a child with big emotions, big energy, and unique challenges—rarely happens in isolation. **It's a team effort.**

And nowhere was that truth more beautifully visible than in one of the most iconic moments of Michael's life—one that had nothing to do with medals and everything to do with love.

Michael had just won his first Olympic gold medal at 19 years old. As the "Star-Spangled Banner" played, he stood tall, took the olive wreath from his head, and pressed it over his heart—just like a baseball player with his cap. It was a beautiful, reverent moment. But something was missing.

As soon as the ceremony ended, Michael pulled out his phone and called his sister Hilary, who was still in the stands with his mom Debbie and sister Whitney.

"Meet me at the fence in ten minutes," he told her.

"Okay, the fence," Hilary said, relaying the plan.

Debbie looked over, curious. "What's going on?" she asked.

"That was Michael," Hilary smiled. "He wants us to meet him at the fence."

A few minutes later, Michael and Bob were on one side of a chain-link fence. Debbie, Hilary, and Whitney were on the other. They were just a few hundred feet from the Olympic pool—but it could have been Debbie's backyard for how grounded, warm, and unguarded that moment felt.

There were no fans. No photographers. No press. Just family. Michael slipped the medal through the fence.

"Mom, look what I did!" he called out, grinning like the little boy she remembered.

Debbie teared up. Hilary and Whitney leaned in close, peeking over her shoulder to see. In that moment, the fence didn't divide them. It connected them.

That medal wasn't just a symbol of athletic greatness. It was a symbol of every drive to practice, every early morning wake-up, every cheer at every meet, and every moment of belief that Team Phelps had poured into his journey.

You don't have to raise an Olympian to have a moment like that. You just have to be the mom who shows up—believing in your child, even when no one else can see what you see. Every act of belief you offer today plants a seed for moments like that—moments where your child looks at you, trophy or not, and says without words: "Look what we did."

> "The strength of the team is each individual member. The strength of each member is the team." – Phil Jackson

Moments like that—where a child feels seen, supported, and celebrated—don't happen by accident. They're built over years of coaching, believing, and steadfast love.

What Great Coaches Really Do

Great coaches understand that building physical strength and stamina is only part of the equation. Exercise, nutrition, and sleep aren't optional—they're essential. Good food fuels growing bodies. Movement strengthens the muscles inside them. Quality sleep helps the brain rest, recover, and synthesize the day's learning.

These aren't just nice extras for athletes. They're must-haves for any child with ADHD.

But physical fundamentals are only the beginning. Because even more important than physical fitness... is mental fitness. So what do great coaches actually do to build that?

They start by building around strengths—not weaknesses. They spot what players do well and place them where they can shine.

They tweak, train, and team up athletes in ways that maximize their natural gifts. They create environments where young people thrive—because they're seen for who they are, not just what they lack.

That's exactly what Coach Bob Bowman did for Michael Phelps. And it's exactly what Michael's mom, Debbie, did too—especially during the difficult school years.

Together, Bob and Debbie formed a united front. They focused on what was working. They built a sturdy, reliable structure around it.

They understood that growth takes rhythm, repetition, and the right amount of challenge—not just wishful thinking. In her book, Debbie shares a glimpse into how she and Bob worked together:

Bob understood the need to weave fun into the grind of long, intense practices. He had a system—after completing their sets, swimmers could jump in the hot tub or play a game. It kept motivation alive.

It worked beautifully for Michael... except when he thought his sets were harder than everyone else's. When that happened, Bob didn't negotiate. The deal was clear: finish the work, then enjoy the reward.

If Michael refused, Bob sent him home early. And Debbie? She backed him up every time.

"Whenever I heard from my son that he needed to be picked up early, I would make him wait until practice was supposed to be over anyway. Michael was never happy about that, but by the time he was fourteen, those moments were happening less and less."

When Michael struggled, his team didn't lower the bar or remove the structure. They stayed steady. The boundaries didn't crumble—they held strong. And over time, those very boundaries became the support Michael needed to build self-discipline and inner motivation.

Debbie puts it this way:

"It turned out that what Michael needed most was structure. We already had swimming, but it could've been any sport or art or structured activity that helped him develop consistency, time on task, and a sense of fun and fulfillment. For anyone searching for that structure, it may take trial and error—but those elements are key."

Michael thrived because his team didn't focus on fixing what was "wrong." They nurtured what was already right—his love for swimming, his competitive fire, his intense focus in the water. They honored his challenges without letting them define him.

Even now, as an adult, Michael continues to reflect on the lasting impact of that support. In the 2020 documentary The Weight of Gold, he reflected on the emotional crisis many Olympians face after the games are over—when years of structure and purpose vanish overnight. Drawing from his own journey, he now champions mental health awareness and emotional resilience for athletes.

So if you've ever asked yourself, "Where do I even begin?" Start with strengths. Then layer in structure and boundaries.

You don't need a fancy plan or expert systems. You just need to strengthen the "Team Coach" inside you—the part that sees what's working and builds from there.

The part that holds firm when your child wants to give up. The part that doesn't just correct—they coach. Because focusing on strengths doesn't just feel more joyful and hopeful—it actually works better.

And when you lead from your child's strengths, you make it more likely that they'll feel capable, confident... and maybe even joyful too.

Here's the best part: You don't have to be a professional coach to build this kind of support. You already have everything you need. You just have to strengthen it—one small, steady choice at a time.

Strengthening Your "Team Coach" Muscle

As a mom of a child with ADHD, I'm guessing you already know your child's challenges inside and out. But here's the bigger question: Do you know their strengths?

Teachers, counselors, and school administrators are trained to assess, document, and focus attention on everything a child struggles with. If your child is falling behind, their weaknesses are placed under a microscope. The lower their test scores, the harsher the spotlight—and often, right behind that glare comes a flood of paperwork: evaluations, special education referrals, IEP meetings, and accommodations.

These systems are well-intentioned. But even when meant to help, they can deliver a damaging, unspoken message: "Here's what's wrong with you."

It gets heavier. The kids struggling academically are often the same ones getting into trouble—called out for being disruptive, inattentive, emotional.

Stack that on top of report cards that don't reflect their real effort—and a parent who feels helpless—and you've got a perfect recipe for anxiety, shame, and a strained parent-child bond.

Maybe your heart is sinking right now—thinking about your child, their struggles, and all the times their efforts have gone unseen.

If so, breathe. You are not alone. You're not failing. You're waking up to what your child truly needs: Not more correction—but more connection.

And one of the simplest, most powerful ways to build that connection? Asking good questions and leading with curiosity instead of correction.

When you lead with questions instead of conclusions, you offer something priceless: The feeling of being seen, heard, and deeply believed in.

"Curiosity is the gateway to connection. When we seek to understand our children instead of fixing them, they finally feel safe enough to grow." – Angel McKim

Why School Can Feel Like a Battle

Is it any wonder so many kids with ADHD grow to hate school?

Let's bring it closer to home. Imagine this is your workday: You show up every day because you have to. You don't love your job, but it's important. Your boss constantly points out everything you're doing wrong:

"You talk too much in meetings."

"Your presentations need work."

You're trying. You're putting in real effort. But it's never enough. You drive home defeated, drained, and wondering how much longer you can keep going. If you've ever felt that way about a job— you already understand your child's experience more than you realize.

Your child doesn't love school either—but they show up because it's important to you. They try hard, but their grades don't reflect it. They get called out for behaviors they don't fully understand. They come home tired, irritable, and discouraged. And the truth is, not every classroom is built to notice their spark.

Some teachers micromanage. Some enforce rules more than they inspire joy. Some mean well but are overwhelmed by a system that values conformity over creativity. But sometimes— sometimes— our kids cross paths with a teacher who sees them.

You'll know when your child finds one. It might be the teacher's natural gift—or a skill they worked hard to build. Either way, your child will remember them forever.

These are the "Team Coaches" inside the classroom. They are the ones who:

- Build trust.

- Offer second chances.

- Teach through relationship, not just rules.

- Remind kids they're more than a grade or a report card.

They notice the spark—and fan it into a flame. If your child hasn't yet had that kind of teacher, you're not imagining it. And it's not their fault—or yours. But here's the good news: The person who knows your child best—the person who can see the spark no one else sees—is *you*.

And here's the even better news: You can be that Team Coach too. In fact, you're already becoming her.

You're learning to shift the focus from what's broken to what's blooming. You're realizing that structure and support can coexist with grace and flexibility. You're seeing that our goal isn't to raise kids who never make mistakes— It's to become their stable, consistent navigator when they do.

"Our goal is not to raise kids that don't make mis-takes—it's to be their sturdy, wise navigator when they do." – Angel McKim

Simple Tools to Strengthen Your Team Coach Muscles

When we focus on contouring, strengthening, and growing our kids' natural abilities, something beautiful happens: Their "gaps" start shrinking on their own. This is the heart of positive psychology—focusing on what's right with us, not just what's wrong.

"The aim of Positive Psychology is to catalyze a change in psychology from a preoccupation only with repairing the worst things in life to also building the best qualities in life." – Martin Seligman, Father of Positive Psychology

If you've ever struggled to spot your child's strengths, you're not alone. The human brain is wired to notice what's wrong—it's a survival instinct called negativity bias. But like any muscle, noticing strengths gets stronger with practice and intention.

Here are a few easy tools to start using right away:

"Three Good Things"

A research-backed strategy to shift focus toward what's going right. At the end of each day, take a moment to jot down three things that made you smile, laugh, or feel connected. They don't have to be big wins—small joys matter most.

Example: "He told a joke at dinner and cracked us all up."

The VIA Character Strengths Survey

Want to discover the hidden strengths you and your child already have? The VIA Institute on Character offers free surveys for adults and kids (ages 8+) that highlight your natural abilities—and how to use them intentionally. Find it at: VIAcharacter.org

Check Your Structure & Boundaries

Ask yourself: Is our structure consistent and predictable? Are our boundaries clear, compassionate, and sturdy enough to handle big emotions? If things feel chaotic or strained, what's one small tweak you could make to help your home feel more grounded?

Assess Your Support Team

Who lifts you up when parenting feels heavy? Who cheers your child on when the world feels hard? Take a moment to reflect: Who's already in your circle? Who could you invite in?

> *"Build a support team that will help you—as you help them." – Bob Bowman, Coach of Michael Phelps*

Finding Balance: Trophy Parent vs. Team Coach

If you've ever found yourself wondering, "Am I helping too much? Not enough? Pushing too hard? Letting too much go?"— you're in good company.

Every mom raising a child with ADHD wrestles with these questions. There's no perfect map for this journey. But there is a compass. And it starts with how we see ourselves—and how we see our kids.

This isn't about labeling ourselves. It's about noticing the patterns we slip into—and gently course-correcting when we need to.

The Trophy Parent

Notices a talent and pressures the child to achieve, often for the parent's validation.

- Success Means...My child wins. I'm proud and feel validated.

- When Failure Happens...Mistakes are met with disappointment or shame.

- What Kids Might Learn..."I'm only lovable when I succeed."

The Team Coach

Helps their child explore, practice, and enjoy their strengths. Balances structure with fun.

- Success Means...My child improves and enjoys the process.

- When Failure Happens...Mistakes are normal. Coach offers support and reflection.

- What Kids Might Learn..."Progress matters more than Perfection."

Academic Fixer

Fixates on weaknesses. Believes success comes from eliminating deficits.

- Success Means...My child gets the right answers and earns the 'A'.

- When Failure Happens...Mistakes are punished. Fun is withheld.

- What Kids Might Learn..."There's only one right way—and I better not mess up."

There's no perfect way to get this right. This table isn't a report card. It's simply a mirror—a gentle reminder that growth is a process.

And every shift you make matters. The real wins are in the trying, not the perfection.

Here's What Matters Most

You don't need to raise an Olympian to be a remarkable mom. You just need to be the one who truly sees your child—especially when others don't. The one who looks past the struggles and spots the potential. The one who doesn't give up, even when the road feels steep and uncertain.

You don't need to have all the answers. You simply need to hold space for growth, offer steady love, and believe—deeply—that your child is more than a diagnosis or a report card.

What mattered most in Debbie Phelps' story wasn't perfection. It was her unwavering belief in her son's strengths. Her willingness to hold boundaries with love. Her decision to coach instead of criticize.

She showed us something powerful: Structure without shame—and support without fixing—is not only possible, it's transformative.

And here's the truth: You can choose this path too. Every time you lead with curiosity instead of judgment, every time you notice a strength instead of a shortcoming, you're reminding your child: You are more than your mistakes.

You're building something that will outlast the struggles. You're building a foundation of belief.

Lead with belief. Build from what's already good. Hold steady when everything feels hard. That's what makes you the coach your child needs—not just today, but for a lifetime.

Because long after they forget the grades, the gold stars, or the trophies... they'll remember you—the mom who never stopped seeing their potential.

"A good coach can change a game. A great coach can change a life." – John Wooden

Want to Add One More Member to Your Team?

You don't have to walk this road alone. I'd be honored to be part of your support circle on this journey.

If you're looking for encouragement, practical tools, or just a space where people truly get it, here are a couple of ways we can connect:

Join my free Facebook community for moms of kids with ADHD

Send me an email at angel@happyrevolutions.com and say hello! I promise I read every single email.

However we connect, know this: I'm in your corner, cheering you on. Every small choice to see their strength, to hold steady with love, is a step toward a brighter future.

And we're just getting started.

CHAPTER 4

The Courage to Believe—Even When the World Doesn't

Coaches build the team. But sometimes, your child needs a Knight Without Armor—someone who chooses belief over fear, even in the face of doubt.

It was the final day of their family vacation. As the sun began to set, Eve and her husband, Ted, were driving home with their young son Richard bouncing around energetically in the back seat—his usual, untamed self. But in this particular moment the chaos hit a tipping point, and Eve snapped.

Without much warning, she screeched the car to a halt about a mile from home and told her son, just six years old at the time, to get out.

"Find your own way home," she said, as Ted looked on, concerned.

Eve was firm and fuming. Ted, who knew Richard's adventurous spirit, suspected he'd rise to the challenge—and he did.

As they abruptly drove away, Richard was left behind to find his way through towering hedges, down a valley, and across the high-grass fields. By today's standards, it was a wild move. But it just might have been the first of many small adventures that shaped Richard into the daring entrepreneur and explorer the world would come to know—Sir Richard Branson. (You know, the

Richard Branson that started Virgin Records, Virgin Atlantic and Virgin Galactic and now offers space flights to civilians.)

Eve later recounted the moment in her memoir, Mum's the Word: The High-Flying Adventures of Eve Branson:

"Looking back on it now, I certainly wouldn't do that again... After an hour, we began to get worried. Dusk was descending. Ted sounded the car horn every five minutes, hoping the noise would give Richard a sense of direction. By 7pm, two hours after we had dropped him off, I was beside myself, realizing my mistake. I remember asking Ted, 'What have I done?' I was frantic."

Finally, around 8pm, the phone rang. A nearby farm had taken in "a little blonde boy who says he's Richard Branson." Sure enough, Richard had found the nearest house, knocked confidently, and waited—completely unfazed. While Eve and Ted were frantic with worry, Richard found the whole adventure thrilling.

Was this the moment that launched him into a life of daring success? Eve wasn't sure. But it was certainly one of many experiences that shaped Richard's fearless spirit and adventurous drive.

As a young mother, Eve firmly believed that children of her time were being raised far too "namby pamby," and she was determined that her own kids would be full of initiative, grit, and self-reliance. She may have gone too far that day—but her instincts were grounded in something deeper: a fierce desire to raise kids who believed they could handle whatever came their way.

Sometimes, the greatest journeys begin with just a little push.

Sir Richard Branson would later come to be known as a real-life Knight without armor.

"The brave may not live forever—but the cautious do not live at all." – Richard Branson, Like a Virgin: Secrets They Won't Teach You at Business School

The Bold Heart Runs in the Family

From an early age, Eve Branson was a woman of bold spirit and relentless drive. At just 14, she packed up and headed to London to train as a ballet dancer—but when World War II broke out, she was determined to do her part. At 19, Eve disguised herself as a boy and joined the Royal Air Force to train as a glider pilot cadet. When her secret was discovered, she didn't stop there—instead, she boldly enlisted in the Women's Royal Naval Service, where she mastered the art of ship signaling from the shadowy edges of Britain's coastlines.

"I got away with an awful lot by being cheeky," she later said. "I just really enjoyed my life."

After the war, Eve became a flight attendant on the first international commercial flights—before cabins were pressurized and comfort was anything but guaranteed. These rocky, altitude-sick flights tested the grit of even the most daring travelers. Eve recounted one of the more harrowing journeys like this:

"The nine-hour flight from Dakar to Brazil proved no smoother than the last leg... As we climbed to 11,000 feet at 230 miles per hour, we passed over the Doldrums to cross the equator. With bumps and jerks, the noise and vibrations threw us all over the cabin while we did our very best to serve our passengers. I myself felt awful. My passengers felt the same. When answering my bell, I found one of them looking ashen and distraught, crying, 'Please stop the plane! I'm scared and I want to get off!'"

When the plane was full, sleep was only possible if you curled up on lumpy mailbags in the cargo hold, jostled by turbulence and exhaustion. It was grueling, but Eve trusted the courageous ex-bomber pilots who'd flown through far worse during the war. They always got her where she needed to go.

In the middle of all life's adventure, Eve met her soulmate, Ted. They quickly married, and soon after, their son Richard was born—followed by daughters Vanessa and Lindy.

It was clear Eve Branson lived a life of courage, grit, and joy. But nowhere did those traits shine more brightly than in her role as a mother. Her devotion to her children ran deep, and her parenting reflected the same daring spirit that once carried her across oceans and through warzones. She raised her children to meet life with boldness, curiosity, and a sense of humor—a legacy of love and adventure that continues to echo through Richard's story even today.

If your child tends to take the long road—or the unexpected one—this next part is for you.

Risk, Resilience, and Real-World Lessons

While Richard's successes are evident today...that was not always the case.

As a young boy, Richard brimmed with boundless energy and curiosity. He was always tinkering with gadgets or dreaming up his next big idea. Eve recognized her son's spark early on—and instead of trying to tame it, she encouraged him to explore it. One year, he planted Christmas trees to sell, only to have them devoured by rabbits. Another time, he tried breeding parakeets.

> *"We don't consider our legacy to be wealth or fame, but the opportunity to pursue happiness by following your own path."—Richard Branson*

That's the kind of legacy we all hope to leave, isn't it?

"He was very conscious that the family had very little money," Eve later said. "We had to try and make money every way we could. It doesn't do you any harm to know what it's like to struggle."

After years of academic struggle with dyslexia and ADHD—and many difficult conversations at home—Richard finally earned his parents' blessing to leave school behind (without graduating) and pursue his dreams. With relentless drive, he launched his first magazine, Student, channeling his passion for writing and giving young people a platform for their voices. But keeping the magazine afloat was financially challenging, and that pressure pushed him to get creative. Soon after, he started his first business selling pop records—naming it Virgin as a nod to his inexperience.

But the road ahead was far from smooth sailing.

At 21, Richard tried skirting purchase taxes on records to save his fledgling business. Customs officials caught on. It was a painful misstep with serious consequences. To bail him out, Eve used the family's only real asset: their home. It was the first time Eve seriously questioned whether she could trust her son's judgment.

She described the moment vividly:

"He was granted bail and released, and we caught the train back to London together, sitting in absolute silence. I could almost hear his mind racing. Crime was out of character for Richard. What he had done was more of a huge risk than anything else. But after what we'd just been through, I felt confident that he was never going to break the law again. It was the best early lesson he could have learned."

While no one can predict the future, looking back now, it's clear how these experiences shaped Richard into the bold entrepreneur—and bold human—he is today.

In his book The Virgin Way, Richard offered Eve a space to reflect, and she didn't hold back:

> *Dear Ricky,*
>
> *We saw it in you from virtually the first moment you began to talk. You were just a toddler, but you clearly liked to do things your own way, on your own terms.*
>
> *You always had some crazy new scheme up your sleeve that you were convinced would change the world—or at least make lots of money. Sometimes your dad and I said, "Oh, don't be ridiculous, Ricky! That's never going to work." But more often, we just let you learn through your mistakes.*
>
> *Your ventures—Christmas trees, bird breeding, all your weird and wonderful ideas—almost always ended in disaster, with us picking up the pieces. But we kept going, hoping those lessons would one day serve you.*
>
> *And they did.*
>
> *After Virgin became a success, we often wondered: what if we'd been more controlling? What if we'd forced you to finish school, like your headmaster at Stowe, who predicted you'd either end up in jail or become a millionaire?*
>
> *In the end, we didn't need to worry. What we thought was stubbornness was really just a budding entrepreneur finding his way. If only we'd known that at the time, we might have had a lot fewer sleepless nights.*
>
> *Love, Mum*

Eve didn't know how Richard's story would turn out. But she never let fear dictate how she showed up. She offered support without smothering his independence. She was bold, curious, and full of grit—even when the future felt uncertain. Eve was the ultimate adventurer in life and motherhood—a true Knight without Armor.

Richard once reflected on his own missteps—and his parents' grace—with this simple truth...

> *"It's so much better, where possible, to try and forgive offenders and give them a second chance—just like my mother and father did so often with me as a child." –* Richard Branson, *The Virgin Way*

Rejecting "Normal," Rewriting the Rules

It was 2019—the year my son was diagnosed with ADHD—and I was desperately trying to find yet another way to help him succeed.

"Now what?" I asked myself. "We've tried everything—meds, parenting classes, diet changes, supplements, neurofeedback. Now what?"

I shuffled across the tile floor to my glowing laptop, ready to dive back into the endless scroll: blog articles, Facebook posts, health message boards. I was looking—again—for the next promising treatment. The next thing to try.

And then I stumbled across a book that would change everything for me.

It was Jonathan Mooney's candid memoir of growing up with dyslexia and ADHD. Today, Jonathan's a multi-award-winning author and outspoken advocate for educational change—but his childhood, by his own account, was anything but successful.

He described how his best friend was the janitor (because he spent more time in the hallway than in the classroom). He knew the school secretary on a first-name basis. Teachers regularly told him he'd "end up flipping burgers or in jail." By the age of 10, Jonathan couldn't read and he was already battling severe anxiety and depression.

His book, *Normal Sucks*, made me shed tears, laugh out loud, and—most of all—question everything I thought I knew about "*normal.*"

But it was his mother, Colleen, who left the deepest impression on me.

One of the earliest things she did—back when Jonathan was still in elementary school and completely drowning—was start something she called *"Get Good at Something Day."* Every Friday, instead of sending Jonathan to school to be torn down again, she took him on an adventure. She gave him opportunities to explore and succeed outside the four walls of a classroom.

She stopped waiting for the system to "fix" him.

That moment cracked something open in me. For the first time, I gave myself permission to stop chasing someone else's version of 'right'. I began to realize how much courage it takes to truly believe in your child—especially when no one else does.

In a 2019 interview with Longreads, Jonathan reflected on the powerful impact of his mom's support. Jonathan didn't sugarcoat the pushback his mom received:

> *"You know, my mom got a ton of shit, man. I mean, there's just no other way to say it. The message to parents of the neurodiverse kid is that their child is deficient, and that their job is to fix their child. We are in a sort of remediation industrial complex, where there's all sorts of services and treatments and interventions to make the square peg fit the round hole. Parents are relentlessly told that that's their job. And my mom rejected that." – Jonathan Mooney*

Maybe you've felt that pressure too—to fix, to correct, to make everything better. But what if your job isn't to fix? What if it's to believe?

Colleen didn't reject support. But she rejected shame. She rejected the idea that her son was broken and needed to be fixed. And so did Jonathan...

"I didn't beat or overcome my 'disability.' My life turned around when I started doing things that focused on my strengths—while also learning to accept my weaknesses."

His story became a north star for me. A reminder that the goal isn't perfection or "fixing" our kids—it's helping them thrive exactly as they are. That our job isn't to eliminate struggle—it's to help our kids build a life of meaning with their differences, not in spite of them.

As Jonathan wrote:

"I had all sorts of labels growing up—bad kid, stupid kid, lazy kid. And eventually I became the special ed, not-normal kid. I had a set of learning and attentional differences that weren't treated as differences. They were treated as deficiencies. So I went on a journey to understand how we've created a culture that values the myth of the normal—instead of the reality of the different."

It takes courage to go against the grain. To advocate when people are judging. To hold on to your child's potential when the world seems intent on shrinking it down.

But maybe, just maybe, the boldest thing you can do is to stop trying to fix your child—and start discovering who they actually are.

> *"Have you ever considered that you are a valuable human being, not despite your differences but because of them?" – Jonathan Mooney, Normal Sucks*

Raising Different Kids Takes a Different Kind of Brave

I'll be honest—this section almost didn't make it into the book. Because part of me thought, "But Jonathan's story is so different from mine. His mom let him skip school for a day of adventure. I'd be terrified to do that."

But that's exactly why it had to stay.

Because the point isn't to become Colleen Mooney. The point is to become the bravest version of you.

Jonathan's mom didn't follow someone else's formula. She made parenting decisions based on her child's actual needs—even when those choices looked "wrong" or "radical" to other people. She trusted herself. She trusted him. And that trust changed everything.

When we're raising kids with ADHD (or any neurodivergence), there are so many voices telling us what to do. Teachers. Doctors. Family. Instagram. Pinterest. That smug mom from car line. And they all seem so sure.

But here's the thing: they don't know your child like you do.

Yes, gather information. Read the books. Learn from others. But don't forget to come back to your own knowing. Because that quiet voice inside of you? It's worth listening to.

You don't need permission to follow a different path. You just need the courage to start walking it.

Building the Courage Muscle—Even When You're Afraid

When your child has ADHD, I believe courage might just be the most essential mental fitness muscle you'll ever need to exercise. Worrying is a natural part of parenting—but chronic worry? That's something different. Constant anxiety doesn't help us, and it definitely doesn't help our kids. Living in fear of what might happen only keeps us stuck in a cycle of stress and second-guessing.

If you or your child struggle with worry, courage isn't just nice to have—it's the antidote.

As moms, we want nothing more than to ease our child's suffering. Our late-night Google sessions, our relentless search for answers, the pile of parenting books on the nightstand—it all comes from love. From the deep desire to fix it. To finally find that one magic solution that will make things better.

But here's the hard truth: sometimes, there is no instant fix. And watching our child struggle—really struggle—is gut-wrenching. We carry not only our child's disappointment, but the phone calls from school, the subtle judgment from other parents, the arguments at home, the fear that we're missing something huge. And it hurts.

So we tell ourselves: "If they could just manage their time..." "If they could just turn in their homework..." "If they could just get it together, then everything would be okay."

But that's a lie. You know it. I know it. We both know moms whose kids are doing all those things—and they're still anxious, still disconnected, still not happy.

Yes, our kids need skills. But can't we build skills and happiness at the same time?

What would happen if, instead of obsessing over every pain point, we strengthened our ability to navigate discomfort? What if we invested just as much energy in expanding our comfort zone as we do trying to shrink our problems?

What if we could breathe through the worry, appreciate their imperfections, and offer them grace instead of guilt?

That's the question I ask myself in those moments when I start spiraling.

You know the ones. Will he graduate high school? Will he ever go to college? Will he be able to hold a job, pay rent, live on his own? What if something happens to me and he can't survive?

Honestly, I've imagined every worst-case scenario—and invented a few more.

I'm a world-class catastrophizer. Maybe you are too.

But then I remember something I learned from Eve Branson—the bold, unconventional mom who helped shape one of the world's most daring entrepreneurs:

What about all the things that could go right?

What might be possible if you trusted your child's light—even when it flickers?

What if our job isn't to fix every flaw—but to be brave enough to follow the joy? To help our kids pursue what lights them up, even if the path looks wildly different from what we expected?

Sometimes courage isn't loud. It's not even visible. Sometimes courage is just a quiet choice: To believe in your child again today. To keep moving forward, even when the outcome isn't clear. To trust that happiness is worth pursuing—even if it means rewriting the plan.

> *"Too many people measure how successful they are by how much money they make or the people that they associate with. In my opinion, true success should be measured by how happy you are."* – Richard Branson

Success isn't about comparison—it's about contentment. Especially for our kids.

Tools and Practical Ways to Stretch Your Brave

Tolerating discomfort takes real courage—especially when it means facing deep-rooted fears or stepping into the unknown on behalf of your child. But courage isn't just for bold, headline-worthy moments. It grows in small ways, in quiet choices, and in everyday parenting decisions where fear is whispering in your ear... and you decide to move forward anyway.

If fear sometimes takes the driver's seat in your parenting (and let's be honest, it happens to the best of us), these small practices might seem simple—but they're powerful. Each time you stretch outside your comfort zone, you strengthen your courage muscle. And just like any muscle, it grows with repetition and intention.

Practice #1: Deep Breathing

Slow, intentional breaths calm your nervous system and give your body the signal: you're safe. When you feel anxious, reactive, or overwhelmed, take three deep breaths—long and slow—and give yourself space to respond instead of react.

Practice #2: Visualization

Picture yourself staying calm during a meltdown. Imagine holding your boundaries with kindness. Visualizing success helps your brain feel more prepared and less threatened, which naturally builds your courage and confidence in real-time moments. (This is a practice Michael Phelps mastered)

Practice #3: Gratitude Shift

When discomfort shows up, fear likes to take the mic. Gratitude turns the volume down. Focus on one thing you're grateful for—right here, right now. It could be your child's laugh, a warm cup of coffee, or the fact that you're still trying. Gratitude is a quiet, steady form of courage.

Practice #4: Small, Brave Steps

Courage doesn't always feel dramatic. It often looks like saying "yes" to something that scares you a little—or saying "no" when everyone expects a "yes." Try one small stretch today. Say the hard thing. Try the new thing. Let your child handle something you usually fix.

One step at a time is how we expand our comfort zone—and teach our kids to do the same.

Becoming the Knight Without Armor

"You don't learn to walk by following rules. You learn by doing and falling over." – Richard Branson

Let this next section guide you away from rule-following and toward brave connection.

This isn't about labeling ourselves. It's about noticing the patterns we slip into—and gently course-correcting when we need to.

The Cowardly Lion

Afraid of everything that could go wrong. Avoids discomfort and risk.

* Success Means...Stick to the safest most familiar path

* When Failure Happens...Feels deep shame and sees mistakes as proof they aren't good enough.

* What Kids Might Learn..."Play it safe because life is full of dangers"

Knight Without Armor

Is vulnerable and afraid but doesn't let fear keep her from taking action.

* Success Means...Embrace discomfort, learn from mistakes and try again.

* When Failure Happens...Views setbacks as part of the process. Adjusts and grows.

* What Kids Might Learn..."Being brave is uncomfortable—but worth it."

The Daredevil

Takes bold risks—sometimes recklessly—that can impact others.

- Success Means...Lives for the thrill of high-risk/high-reward outcomes.

- When Failure Happens...May ignore consequences, risking burnout, harm or lost trust.

- What Kids Might Learn..."I'm invincible. Rules don't apply to me."

Here's What Matters Most

Courage isn't loud. It's not always brave-sounding. Sometimes, it looks like holding your child's pain in one hand and your love for them in the other—and choosing to keep going, even when you're not sure where the road leads.

It looks like questioning the system. Saying no to shame. Trusting your gut when everyone else says, "Fix them." It looks like choosing connection over compliance. Choosing joy over perfection. Choosing the longer, messier, more meaningful path—because it's the one where your child can actually flourish.

You don't need to raise a billionaire or a world-changer. You just need to raise a child who knows—deep in their bones—that they are believed in.

Because when you believe in them—even when the world doesn't—you give them the courage to believe in themselves.

That is your legacy. That is your magic. That is the power of becoming a Knight Without Armor.

And the beautiful part? You don't need to feel brave to be brave. Just keep showing up. That's enough.

> *"Courage is what it takes to stand up and speak; courage is also what it takes to sit down and listen." – Richard Branson, The Virgin Way*

CHAPTER 5

Raising a Child Who Learns to Talk to Themselves Like a Friend

Extreme Childhood – Where chaos reigned, creativity took root.

What do you get when you mix a tornado with a hurricane? Ty Pennington's childhood—that's what. While the popular designer and TV personality is now known for his charming smile and infectious energy, few people realize just how chaotic his early years really were. Behind that winning grin was a boy who could barely sit still long enough to stay out of trouble.

His mom, Yvonne, had her hands full. A powerhouse of grit and perseverance, she worked full-time, attended college, and raised two energetic boys—Ty and his older brother, Wynn. But no degree or parenting book could have prepared her for the whirlwind that was Ty.

Ty's path to fame as America's favorite carpenter and host of Extreme Makeover: Home Edition might look like a straight shot from talent to success. But back then? Yvonne would have described it less like an "extreme success" and more like an "extreme mess."

In his memoir, Life to the Extreme: How a Chaotic Kid Became America's Favorite Carpenter, Ty recounts a moment that perfectly captures the essence of his early childhood. One day, his mom—then a graduate student working toward her doctorate in child psychology—showed up at his elementary school and asked the principal if she could observe "the worst kid in the class" for her research.

Ty remembers what happened next:

The principal thinks this must be some kind of weird joke—but it's not. She's dead serious. And when she peers through the glass into the classroom to observe that terrible, disruptive kid? That's me. I'm the one she's looking at.

There I am, ducking incoming fire in the form of paper airplanes, launching erasers like grenades, dragging my desk around the classroom corridor like it's a tank. I'm using the teacher's pets as shields. I'm completely naked. This is why I was dragging the desk—I was trying to cover up my "homework." You should've seen the substitute teacher's face.

Yvonne stood there, frozen in horror, as Ty stripped naked, "wore" his desk like armor, and swung from the classroom blinds. It was total chaos—but Ty was absolutely thriving in it. Why pay attention to a lecture on the water cycle when anarchy was so much more fun?

But this wasn't a one-off incident. Ty didn't "grow out of" his ADHD. He just grew into more inventive—and sometimes destructive—ways of channeling it. He jumped off rooftops pretending to be in the army, got kicked out of Boy Scouts for biting a kid's ear, set fire to the woods (then lied about it), and routinely found himself in trouble.

Yvonne, like many moms of kids with ADHD, tried everything to support her son. She discovered that certain activities—drawing, puzzles, and sports—helped him regulate and focus. Ty especially loved soccer and art, and Yvonne made sure those passions were nurtured. His artwork filled the refrigerator not just because she was proud, but because she knew it represented something more: his potential.

She refused to let the world write him off.

She didn't see a troublemaker—she saw a work of art in progress.

> *"Every person out there with ADHD has a hidden talent that they must find, because it's the confidence that you can gain from that [discovery] that's life-changing." –*
> *Ty Pennington*

Extreme Darkness – When behavior labels stick harder than encouragement.

> *"I think a lot of people don't understand how much of an impact this condition [ADHD] has on a person, and what a struggle it can be in your life—not just in your grades and your job, but with your relationships. Especially when you're a teen, people are trying to understand what's going on with you and you just don't have a good way to really communicate it." –* Ty Pennington, Ability Magazine, 2007

When Ty entered high school, he kept playing soccer and channeling his creativity into art. But by the time he arrived at Cross Keys High School, his reputation had beaten him there. Teachers already knew about the chaos he'd stirred up back at Ashbury Park Elementary. They had him pegged before he even walked through the door.

Here's how Ty remembers it:

"This is what I figured out about teachers. In elementary school, you have sweet teachers who think, 'I love my job and I love my kids.' But in high school, the teachers are so burnt out by troublemakers like me that they're basically like, 'You know what? I don't have time for you. You're a little turd—go stand in the hallway so I can focus on the kids who want to learn.'"

At Cross Keys, Ty had already been slapped with labels like "special needs" and "learning disabled"—words that made him furious.

"Learning disabled? I'll punch your face!" he writes. "Everybody in the hallway sees me as the problem child. The only solution is to move to a different county—and a different school—because otherwise, you end up in a correctional school. One step away from juvie."

As Ty entered his turbulent teen years, he wasn't just barely surviving school—he was unraveling. Soccer stopped working for him, and with that anchor gone, everything began to tailspin. His grades plummeted, his relationships fractured, and worst of all, he started to lose touch with himself.

"I go through some very tough years—very violent, angry years—where I want to fight everybody, including people in my own family."

He turned his bedroom into a chaotic creative lab—tearing apart household items to make art. But the darkness inside him seeped into his sketches, and one day, it was too much for his mom.

Yvonne stood at his doorway, holding up his latest drawing—rats pulling wagons full of severed fingers.

"Okay, that's it," she said, concern etched across her face. "*You're getting help.*"

Ty didn't understand what the big deal was. This was just his way of working through the chaos. It was his dark phase. It was art. But Yvonne trusted her gut.

She took him to see Dr. Gaston Loomis, a psychiatrist in Atlanta. Dr. Loomis was quirky and brilliant—he had Ty sit and eat candy while they talked. And then, like it was the most obvious thing in the world, Dr. Loomis turned to Yvonne and said:

"Your son is the poster child for ADHD."

He should know. He had it himself.

That moment was a revelation for Ty. Someone smart. Someone successful. Someone just like him. For the first time, Ty saw that having ADHD didn't mean being broken. It meant being different—and capable.

With that new perspective, Ty enrolled in Kennesaw Community College—and there, something else happened that changed everything.

He received *encouragement.*

"I'm taking an art history class and doing well, and one day the art teacher pulls me aside." 'You realize you're talented, right?' she asks. 'I guess,' I say, not sure how serious she is. 'No, I'm serious. There are a lot of students who come in here and can draw. But you've got it. I'd hate for you to waste that.'

That tiny moment of belief—the kind he'd rarely experienced in school—sparked something. Ty started looking into jobs in the art world. He began charting a path. For the first time, the future didn't feel like a minefield. It felt like a canvas.

"One word of encouragement can be enough to spark someone's motivation to continue with a difficult challenge." – Roy T. Bennett

Extreme Commitment – The power of a mom who believes—and keeps believing

By his own admission, Ty didn't grow up with a lot of boundaries or structure. What he did grow up with, though, was something just as powerful: a mom who refused to give up on him. Yvonne may not have had the perfect parenting plan, but she showed up with unshakable perseverance and an unbreakable belief in her son.

Ty describes her like this:

"A person whose passion for working, learning, loving, and laughing is matched only by their excitingly infectious, hilarious personality. A person who can help you learn and learn to love yourself at the same time."

"She was the ultimate do-it-yourselfer. A waitress, a student, a teacher, a parent, a psychologist, a professional, a dancer, a wife, and a mother—all at once. She could juggle almost anything (except cats...she's highly allergic). She was what you might call driven."

So what part of Yvonne made the biggest difference for Ty?

Yes, she had grit. Yes, she was resourceful. But more than anything, it was this: she believed in her son—even when the world didn't. She tuned out the noise from teachers who doubted him, the tension at home with his brother and stepfather, and the critical voice in her own head. She didn't let the chatter define her parenting. She kept going. She kept learning. She focused on progress, not perfection.

That kind of strength is quiet but fierce. And Ty felt it.

But while Yvonne could tune out the critics, Ty struggled to do the same. His inner critic was loud, persistent, and mean. And when things got dark, Yvonne knew she couldn't do it alone. She called in support. She built her team.

She took Ty to Dr. Loomis—the psychiatrist who would help Ty reframe how he saw himself. With Dr. Loomis, Ty began learning how to spot his unhelpful thoughts, quiet his inner critic, and speak to himself more kindly. Yvonne wanted to make sure her son had more than survival skills. She wanted him to develop real tools for mental fitness—tools to navigate the world with confidence, emotional regulation, and self-belief.

"Sometimes you need more than a dream to turn that opportunity into success...you need hard work, determination, a competitive edge, a passion, a drive for perfection and excellence. But most importantly, you need what we all need: Someone who believes in you. And that person needs to be you. – Ty Pennington, Commencement Speech, Savannah College of Art and Design, 2012

The Ventriloquist – Teaching your child to become their own best encourager

Tell a stranger that you talk to yourself, and you're likely to get written off as eccentric. But the truth is, we all have a voice in our head—and so do our kids. That internal voice can be a game-changer. When things get hard, we hope to hear our inner coach cheering us on. But too often, it's the inner critic who shows up first.

When we're facing a challenge, our inner coach says: "You can do this. You've got this." But our inner critic? "I'm going to fail. I suck. Everyone's going to laugh. Why even try?"

Sometimes that voice becomes so loud—and so familiar—we stop noticing it altogether.

And then we wonder why we don't feel confident.

It's because, over time, we start believing what we think. Without even realizing it, we let these thugs of thought take over. They sneak in like masked bandits, quietly stealing our confidence, courage, and sense of worth. Left unchecked, these mental outlaws can wreak havoc on our self-esteem and mental health.

So here's a simple but powerful question: If your friend came to you feeling down, how would you talk to them? Would you criticize them for struggling? Call them stupid for making a mistake?

Of course not.

So why do we talk to ourselves that way?

There could be a mile-long list of reasons: comparison, perfectionism, shame, pressure to fit into impossible standards. Maybe someone in your past made you feel small—and that voice stuck. But whatever the reason, we don't have to keep letting that voice run the show.

Instead of letting our minds wander to the barren desert of comparisons, we can learn to redirect them—to the oasis of replenishment and compassion. That starts with noticing what we're telling ourselves. It starts with catching the thought thugs in action and choosing not to let them run the show anymore.

We want happy, confident kids. But how we treat ourselves teaches them how to treat themselves.

When we learn to speak to ourselves like we would a best friend... When we believe in ourselves with the same fierce energy we pour into our children... When we model compassion, grace, and self-respect...That's when our kids learn to believe in themselves, too.

> *"Do not allow negative thoughts to enter your mind, for they are weeds that strangle confidence." – Bruce Lee*

Helping your child catch their thought-thieves—and talk back with love

Unfortunately, it's not uncommon to hear a child with ADHD say things like, "I'm stupid," "I'm dumb," or "I just can't." And honestly, it's not surprising. Our culture is full of confidence-sucking potholes—especially for kids with ADHD. Every day, our kids are slamming into these potholes: every comparison to their peers, every failed attempt, every correction or redirection. And just like a car getting battered by the road, they break down.

That's why they need tools—to make repairs and keep going. And even more importantly, they need the skills to dodge those potholes in the future.

In his book *Chatter: The Voice in Our Head, Why It Matters, and How to Harness It*, psychologist Ethan Kross shares his research and personal stories about managing our internal dialogue. It's all about turning that inner critic into a source of strength. With the right tools, you and your child can transform that mental chatter into something far more helpful—a voice that builds confidence, instead of breaking down.

So go ahead—experiment. Try these tools and see what works for you and your child:

Distanced Self-Talk

Put a little distance between you and your thoughts. Instead of saying, "I'm so overwhelmed," say, "[Your Name] is feeling overwhelmed right now." This simple shift helps you step back, see the bigger picture, and get out of the emotional storm. It works for kids, too. Try modeling it for them or helping them find words for what they're feeling.

Example: "Carrie is feeling depleted right now. She needs a reset."

Advise a Friend

Talk to yourself the same way you'd talk to a friend—with kindness, perspective, and compassion. Use your name as if you're coaching yourself through it.

"Angel, let's go for a walk and take a break. You've been working hard—everyone needs a reset sometimes."

Write Expressively

Take 15 minutes a day for three days to journal about something that's been weighing on you. Write in the third person like a neutral observer. Research shows this helps reduce rumination and makes your thoughts easier to work with.

Mental Time Travel

Zoom out. How will this moment feel in a week, a month, or a year? This perspective shift can shrink today's worries down to size and help you or your child focus on what really matters.

You don't need fancy tools or clinical techniques to change your inner dialogue. You just need a willingness to try—and a little bit of practice.

"Of course I talk to myself. Sometimes I need expert advice." – Unknown

When your child can't believe in themselves yet, they borrow your belief

Let this next section be your permission slip to pause and reflect.

Not to critique yourself—but to notice how your inner voice leads, comforts, or sometimes criticizes—and to begin rewriting that story with kindness.

> ## The Chatter box
>
> Constantly compares self to others in unhelpful ways. Allows intrusive thoughts to take over.
> - Success Means...Can celebrate wins, but self-doubt quickly creeps in with the next challenge.
>
> - When Failure Happens...Spirals into self-loathing. Harsh inner critic takes over.
>
> - What Kids Might Learn..."My thoughts define me. I'll never be good enough."

> ## The Ventriloquist
>
> Talks to self like a trusted friend. Gives calm, wise guidance.
> - Success Means...Notices unhelpful thoughts and replaces them before they spiral. Can self-soothe and stay grounded.
>
> - When Failure Happens...Uses distanced self-talk to shift perspective and keep going. Tries again with curiosity and care.
>
> - What Kids Might Learn..."I'm not my thoughts. I can handle hard things and keep learning."

The Egotist

Craves admiration. Believes worth is tied to status, success, or attention.

- Success Means...Brags about successes for approval. Lacks awareness of deeper insecurity underneath.

- When Failure Happens...Becomes overly concerned with how failure reflects on them. May project blame or shut down.

- What Kids Might Learn..."My job is to impress others. My own needs and feelings don't matter as much."

Here's what Matters Most

You don't need to raise the world's most charming TV host to know what it's like to have a child who feels like a tornado in a quiet room. You don't need a child with a hammer and power tools to know what it's like to live on high alert—hoping today is the day things go a little smoother, hoping your child sees what you see: their strength, their potential, their heart.

Ty Pennington's story isn't just one of success—it's one of redemption. It's a story of a boy who couldn't sit still and a mom who refused to sit down when it came to fighting for him. Yvonne didn't always get it right, but she got the most important thing right: she believed in her son—even when the world didn't. And when her belief wasn't enough, she brought in help. She didn't just teach Ty to quiet the noise in his head—she helped him learn how to believe in himself.

You may not be able to change your child's wiring, but you can change what they believe about it.

You can teach them that they're not broken. That their wild ideas matter. That their brain isn't a problem to solve—it's a blueprint to work with. You can show them how to tame their inner critic and tune into their inner coach. You can help them understand that they're not their worst moments—and neither are you.

So when it feels hard—and it will—don't forget this:

You're the one who sees what's possible. You're the one who can make space for repair. You're the one who helps your child believe they're not "the problem."

You are not raising a problem to fix. You are raising a person to love.

And when they finally believe it too... everything begins to change.

The Hostage Negotiator

You've seen what fierce belief looks like in the lives of high-profile moms. But some of the most powerful shifts happen in everyday homes—without the spotlight. This is one of those stories.

From Tension to Escape: When Conflict Breaks Connection

Janet Riddle was a 42-year-old realtor living in middle-class suburbia. She had three kids—two boys and one girl. While her sons seemed to breeze through school, her daughter, Kristen, now 14, had struggled from the very beginning. Janet had tried everything—tutors, medication, alternative curricula, behavioral therapy—desperate for Kristen to feel successful again. But nothing seemed to stick.

And slowly, heartbreakingly, the struggle didn't just stay at school. It followed them home and started taking over everything. The battles over schoolwork seeped into dinner time, bedtime, even weekends.

Kristen hated school—but at least at school, she got a break from her mom's constant stream of corrections, commands, and concerns. At home, the air felt heavy with tension. Most conversations with her mom spiraled into arguments about homework, grades, or all the things Kristen wasn't doing right.

Though she wouldn't have used the word, Kristen was starting to feel like a hostage in her own home—emotionally cornered by constant correction.

It wasn't until their already fragile relationship hit a new low that Janet finally reached out for professional help—hoping someone, anyone, could offer a lifeline.

But Janet didn't know Kristen had already made a decision of her own. She was going to run.

Why She Ran—and Why So Many Kids Want To

It was a sunny Friday afternoon in Florida. Kristen was in the back-yard, laughing as she chased her younger brother Kyle through the grass, their giggles bouncing off the fence. Janet was inside on a work call, focused on a client. Everything seemed normal—until a black car pulled up near the side yard. Kristen, without a word, walked over to the car and got in.

No suitcase. No goodbye. Just the slam of a car door and the sound of tires crunching gravel as she disappeared.

Kyle froze.

He wasn't panicked. Just confused. It didn't make sense—Kristen didn't even say goodbye. He wandered back into the house, unsure of what he'd just seen. He waited patiently until Janet was finished with her work call and jumped in:

"Mom, where's Kristen going?" he asked.

"What do you mean?" Janet replied, eyebrows knitting together.

"I don't know... she just got in some black car with people."

"What are you talking about?" Janet muttered, now standing.

As Kyle continued describing what happened, the room tilted. Janet's heart thundered, her hands fumbling for her phone. Her thoughts scattered like leaves in a storm. She called Kristen. Straight to voicemail. She tried again. Still nothing.

Within minutes, she was texting Kristen's friends, calling parents, scrolling through contacts—anything to make sense of what was happening.

As the hours passed and Kristen didn't return home, the dread settled in. Janet posted to her neighborhood's Facebook group, asking if anyone had seen a black car. Then came the calls to the police. The social media posts. The missing person report.

By the next morning, Kristen's photo was on a "Missing Juvenile" bulletin. Her name and face spread quickly. Within hours, the neighborhood message boards lit up—some offering encouragement, some reporting possible sightings, others casting blame. The whole ordeal turned into a digital wildfire.

Through it all, Janet clung to one fragile thread: that her daughter would come home—not just safe, but still willing to come back to her.

But it wasn't that simple. Messages poured in. Kristen had been seen around town—and some local families were even letting her stay over, ignoring Janet's pleas and the fact that her daughter was listed as a missing person.

Four days later, Kristen walked into a local police station and turned herself in. She was safe. Unharmed. But something had undeniably cracked open.

A few days later, Janet quietly deleted her posts. The social media frenzy died down just as quickly as it had started. And the family began doing what they needed to do:

Retreat. Regroup. Rebuild.

For Janet, this wasn't just a turning point in her daughter's life—it was the wake-up call that something in their dynamic needed to change. Not with stricter rules, but with stronger connection.

If you're raising a child with ADHD, you've probably had moments where connection feels impossible—where every request becomes a battle, every conversation turns tense, and your child pulls further away. You're not trying to fight. You're trying to connect. But in those moments, it can feel like you're talking someone off a ledge. That's why learning to think like a hostage negotiator isn't as strange as it sounds—it's one of the most powerful tools we have.

"If you live your life as a hostage to everybody else's decision, you either have to live a very narrow life, or you have to spend a lot of time in pain." – Newt Gingrich

The Accidental Hostage Taker

The first time I compared parenting a child with ADHD to hostage negotiation, one of my coaching clients laughed out loud.

"That's ridiculous," he said. He was the dad of a 13-year-old adopted son—brilliant, but quick to explode. A kid with a biting sense of humor, a strong will, and a short fuse.

I smiled. "Is it, though?" I asked. "Have you ever tried negotiating homework, bedtime, or screen time with a dysregulated child?"

Most of the moms I work with face some version of this: a child who's disinterested, defiant, or emotionally flooded. The conversation starts calm—and then suddenly, it's a standoff.

Like so many of us, I didn't grow up knowing how to stay calm in chaos—or how to hold space for someone else's big emotions without losing my own. My parents didn't have those tools either. And when no one teaches us how to navigate disagreement, we usually do one of two things: avoid it—or make it worse.

> *"The reality is that most of us communicate the same way that we grew up. That communication style becomes our normal way of dealing with issues—our blueprint. It's what we know and pass on to our own children. We either become our childhood or we make a conscious choice to change it." – Kristen Crockett*

And the truth is, almost everything is a negotiation. Getting out the door in the morning. Getting your child to brush their teeth. Talking about chores, homework, screen time. Childhood is full of constant change—and that means it's full of conflict. But conflict doesn't have to be chaos. With the right tools, it can also be connection.

Growing up, I never ran away from home. But I have felt the burn in my chest, the sting of un-shed tears and the magnetic pull of the front door—just to escape the weight of being misunderstood.

That feeling—the ache of not being seen or heard—is at the heart of the three core reasons kids run away, according to the Missing Children's Network:

- Poor or nonexistent communication with parents

- A lack of emotional tools to manage stress and conflict

- Emotional, verbal, or physical harm from trusted adults

These things don't just lead to runaway moments—they lead to relationships where both parent and child feel like hostages.

But here's the hard truth and hopeful news: mastering negotiation changes everything. It builds bridges instead of walls. It can turn your home into a place of rest from the world—not a source of stress inside it.

"When parenting feels like a standoff, connection—not control—is your way through." – Angel McKim

Becoming the Steady Voice Your Child Can Count On

Some parents hear the word negotiation and immediately bristle. It sounds like giving in. Like losing control.

They usually say: "If I start negotiating with my kid, they'll think they run the show."

But here's the truth: you're already negotiating with your child—all the time. Whether it's a bedtime battle, a screen-time standoff, or a morning meltdown over socks, you're in the middle of constant micro-negotiations. And for moms raising kids with ADHD, those negotiations can feel especially exhausting.

Many of us think of negotiation as something that happens in the boardroom. You picture a job interview, a contract discussion, maybe a big ask at work. But some of the most important negotiations of your life are happening at your kitchen table. In your car. At the foot of your child's bed after a hard day.

Negotiation is just communication. It's not about who wins—it's about staying connected while solving problems. When we negotiate with empathy and clarity, it becomes one of our most powerful parenting tools.

"Life is a series of negotiations you should be prepared for: buying a car, negotiating a salary, buying a home,

*renegotiating rent, deliberating with your partner." –
Chris Voss, former FBI hostage negotiator*

In his bestselling book *Never Split the Difference*, Voss shares
tools that helped him navigate high-stakes, high-emotion stand-
offs—skills that, surprisingly, apply just as well to families as they
do to fugitives. His approach blends empathy with emotional regulation, and if you've ever tried to reason with a dysregulated child,
you already know how valuable that combo can be.

Because parenting a child with ADHD isn't just high-stakes—it's
high-emotion. Our kids struggle with impulse control, emotional
regulation, and flexible thinking. Which means we, as parents,
have to work twice as hard to stay grounded and guide the storm
instead of getting swept up in it.

That's why the hostage negotiation metaphor works. Not because our kids are criminals, but because the strategies used in
a life-or-death crisis also happen to work beautifully in everyday
moments of chaos—when emotions are running high, and connection feels like it's slipping through our fingers.

*"What you want to do is put people in a position where
they feel connected enough to you that they're willing to
collaborate... willing to show you the things they were
scared to tell you about before." – Chris Voss*

Strengthening Your Negotiating Muscles

"Negotiation is the art of letting the other side have it your way" – *Christopher Voss, former FBI hostage negotiator and author*

You may have heard experts warn: "Stop negotiating with your kids!" As if the very act of listening and collaborating is the gateway to chaos.

But the truth is, negotiation done well doesn't weaken your authority—it builds your connection. It strengthens trust, teaches problem-solving, and helps your child practice the real-life skills they'll need again and again.

Negotiation isn't about giving in. It's about leaning in. It's not about letting your child win. It's about helping them feel heard—so they're open to solutions instead of stuck in resistance.

Because the best hostage negotiators don't scream or slam doors. They stay calm, build trust, and choose connection over control. And that's exactly what parenting a child with ADHD asks us to do—*over and over* again.

I don't know what happened to Janet and Kristen. She's not a household name or someone on a stage. She's just a mother whose love for her daughter nearly broke her—and who still chose to stay soft, stay open, and try again. There are countless moms like her—women who love fiercely but whose children feel trapped, unheard, or unseen beneath the weight of their challenges. Janet's name may never appear in headlines, but her story echoes the quiet heartbreak and courage of thousands of mothers, making it one of the most important to tell.

So if you've ever found yourself in Janet's shoes—trying to connect but watching your child pull away—let's look at what can help.

The Teeter-Totter

The first job of any negotiator? Lower the emotional heat. Educators often use a simple image to explain it—a teeter-totter. On one side: emotion. On the other: rational thinking. When one side goes up, the other drops.

As Gary Noesner, former chief of the FBI's Crisis Negotiation Unit, explains: "The most damaging thing for a negotiator is losing self-control. If you can't manage your own emotions, how can you influence someone else's?"

And he's right. It's normal to get triggered when your child is melting down, breaking rules, or ignoring directions. But inflamed emotions make connection harder—and negotiation almost impossible. A hostage negotiator doesn't get to yell and walk away. Neither do we when our relationship with our child is on the line.

Tactical Empathy

This is where tactical empathy comes in. It's not manipulation. It's not weakness. It's a powerful skill for disarming big emotions and building trust.

Chris Voss defines tactical empathy as becoming "utterly aware of the other person's perspective." It's stepping into their world—not to agree with everything—but to understand it. And that feeling of being understood? It shifts everything.

> *"The moment you've convinced someone that you truly understand her dreams and feelings, mental and behavioral change becomes possible, and the foundation for a breakthrough has been laid." – Chris Voss*

Labeling

One of the fastest ways to defuse emotion is to name it. Labeling helps your child feel seen without needing to defend themselves. It's a simple sentence starter like:

"It seems like you're feeling ____."

"It looks like you're really ___ right now."

"It sounds like you're ____."

"It feels like you're ____."

Let's say your 8-year-old refuses to eat dinner unless you tell her a story. Instead of going straight to "no," try: "It sounds like you love stories at dinner." You've now acknowledged her need, which makes it easier to offer a compromise like: "I'll tell one after we eat."

If she's still upset? Try: "It sounds like you're frustrated." You may need a few labels to help her settle, but each one is helping her return to calm.

Labeling isn't just about managing behavior. It's about deepening connection. It says, "I see you. I get it. I'm here."

Mirroring

Another simple, powerful tool? Mirroring. Just repeat back one to three words your child says—as a question. It shows you're listening and invites them to keep talking.

"Can I go to Jimmy's party?"

"Jimmy's party?"

"Yeah, at his grandparents' beach house this weekend."

"Beach house?"

"They're letting him throw a graduation party. He's a senior."

Now you've learned something important: Jimmy's a senior, your son is a sophomore, and the situation might not be appropriate. But instead of shutting it down, you've gathered insight—and created space for your child to think critically about the situation.

Mirroring helps your child hear their own reasoning—and helps you respond with wisdom instead of reactivity.

"Trust is earned in the smallest of moments. It is earned not through heroic deeds, or even highly visible actions, but through paying attention, listening, and gestures of genuine care and connection." – Brene Brown

Replace "Why" with "What" and "How"

Another favorite strategy of Chris Voss: drop the word "why."

"Why" questions trigger defensiveness—especially in kids. Instead of asking, "Why didn't you clean your room?", try:

"What needs to happen so your room gets cleaned before dinner?"

"How can I help you make this part of your routine?"

"What" and "how" invite collaboration.

They shift the focus from blame to problem-solving—and help your child feel more capable and in control.

A Real-Life Example

In one of his most famous cases, Chris Voss spent six hours speaking through a door in a Harlem apartment. Inside were three heavily armed fugitives. He didn't threaten. He didn't escalate.

He used empathy.

"It looks like you don't want to come out."

"It seems like you're afraid of going back to jail."

Over time, the fugitives calmed. They felt understood. And eventually, they surrendered peacefully.

The takeaway? Empathy doesn't make you weak. It makes you effective.

We don't master negotiation overnight. These are skills. They take practice—just like reading, math, or riding a bike.

But tactical empathy? Labeling? Mirroring? Replacing "why" with "what"? These tools help you build trust, co-regulate emotions, and model exactly what your child needs most. What better gift could you give?

Because every child wants to be heard. Even when they don't have the words. Even when they're yelling, slamming doors, or saying things they don't mean.

Every child wants to be understood. And you can be the one who shows them how.

Everyday Practices for Raising Emotionally Safe Kids

Negotiation is one of the most powerful skills you can model—especially when raising a child with ADHD. It's not just about resolving conflict in the moment. It's about building skills your child will use for the rest of their life, including:

- Solving problems through collaboration

- Strengthening self-awareness

- Learning to communicate wants and needs

- Understanding other perspectives

Negotiation isn't about winning or losing. It's about learning how to work together—to listen, reflect, and move forward with connection intact. That's not just good for your child's future. It's good for your relationship now.

What would happen if you tried...

Slowing Things Down

Instead of powering through a conflict, hit pause. Let emotions settle so clarity can return. This helps both of you come back to the conversation with more calm and capacity.

Watching Your Tone

Even when the words are calm, tone can make them sharp. Breathe. Slow down. Practice speaking in a calm, open tone—even when you're setting firm boundaries.

Noticing Your Body Language

Your posture, gestures, and eye contact all send signals. Open, grounded body language signals safety—and helps your child stay in the conversation instead of shutting down.

Practicing Conflict Resolution

Look for everyday chances to flex this muscle—at work, at home, in hard conversations. Practice looking beneath the behavior—and finding a way forward together.

Studying Negotiation Techniques

There are tons of books, podcasts, and bite-sized resources to help you grow this skill—including Chris Voss's Never Split the Difference. Explore what resonates.

Seeking Feedback

After tricky conversations, reflect. What worked? What didn't? If it feels safe, ask your child how they felt. Growth doesn't require perfection—just a willingness to keep learning.

"Body language and tone of voice - not words - are our most powerful assessment tools." – Chris Voss

Three Parenting Archetypes: Which One Shows Up in You?

Let this next section help you see the patterns that surface under stress—without shame or self-blame.

This isn't about judging yourself. It's about recognizing when control takes the driver's seat so you can choose connection instead.

The Scrooge

Withdraws emotionally. Expects kids to manage big feelings alone.

- Success Means...Obedience and perfection. Mistakes = failure.

- When Failure Happens...Responds with shame, punishment, or disconnection.

- What Kids Learn..."My big feelings are a problem—and I'm on my own."

The Hostage Negotiator

Stays grounded in chaos. Leads with empathy and clear limits.

- Success Means...Emotional safety, mutual respect, and steady connection.

- When Failure Happens...Pauses. Repairs. Reconnects with intention and care.

- What Kids Learn..."It's okay to feel big things. I can ask for help and stay connected.

The Hostage Taker

Uses power to control. Reacts from frustration, not connection.

- Success Means...Total compliance. Control = success.

- When Failure Happens...Doubles down on threats, yelling, or sarcasm.

- What Kids Learn..."I have to shut down or push harder to be heard."

Here's What Matters Most

You don't need to stop every battle. You don't need the perfect script. You don't even need to be the calmest person in the room all the time.

But you do have the power to shift the tone.

When emotions run high, your presence—steady, open, and grounded—can be the anchor your child clings to. The tone you set becomes the tone they learn to use with themselves. That's the real win—the one that lasts.

Because when you stop trying to control every outcome and start focusing on connection—you become the negotiator your child needs most. Not the one with ultimatums, but the one who listens deeply. The one who helps them come back to calm. The one who helps them think again when big feelings flood their body.

You don't need to yell louder. Or fix it faster. Or hold it all alone.

You don't have to have all the answers. You just need to hold steady. Because your calm presence? It becomes the voice they carry inside—the one that says: I can come back. I'm safe to try again.

> *"Courage is what it takes to stand up and speak. Courage is also what it takes to sit down and listen." –*
> *Winston Churchill*

This isn't caving. It's teaching your child that conflict doesn't have to mean disconnection.That emotions aren't threats. And that healthy negotiation—where both people feel seen—can be one of the greatest gifts you give them.

Especially in a world that doesn't always listen.

CHAPTER 7

The Clean Sweep

When Holding It Together Starts to Hurt

Last chapter, we met The Hostage Negotiator—the version of you that can stay calm in chaos, connect under pressure, and defuse storms with empathy. But here's the truth: even the best negotiator loses her footing when the emotional weight gets too heavy. You can only keep the peace for so long before the pressure inside you starts to build. And if you never get a chance to step away—to release it, to breathe—eventually, that pressure has nowhere to go but out.

That's what this chapter is about. Because sometimes, the emotional garbage we're carrying catches fire—and when it does, it's the people we love most who get burned. I know, because I've been there. And if you have too, you're not alone.

Let me take you back to a regular morning—the kind we all know too well—that turned into a breaking point I never saw coming.

Before we dive in, just know—if you've ever lost it, it doesn't make you a bad mom. It makes you human.

"Some mornings it feels like I'm juggling everyone's needs with one hand—and my sanity with the other." – Angel McKim

The Juggle Is Real

It's no small task to be a mom—working or otherwise. I look back with a mix of awe and disbelief at all those chaotic mornings, plucking my kids from their warm, comfy beds just to get us out the door for work—without killing each other.

If you've ever stood in a doorway, coffee in one hand and chaos in the other, wondering how you'll get through another morning—you know the mix of love and exhaustion that lives there. That breath between patience and panic? That's the real mom battleground.

When my kids were really little, I remember showing up to work still fully wearing my "mom hat." One time, I arrived with my shirt on inside out and didn't even notice until a kind coworker pointed out the tag fluttering in the breeze as I walked down the hall. Another time, my top was on backwards—and I didn't realize until it started choking me like a toddler carrying a cat by the head.

Let's just say, I wasn't showing up to work in polished pumps and perfectly pressed suits. My shoes were more likely to be covered in baby spit-up than shoe polish. And those were just the mornings.

Throughout the day, I shifted seamlessly (or not-so-seamlessly) into whatever role was needed. At work, I was the project manager, the leader, the organizer, the team cheerleader. But when the workday ended, my real shift began: the role of Mom. And Mom wears a lot of hats.

> *"I'm the glue holding everything together—and sometimes, I'm the one cracking underneath it." – Anonymous Mom*

You remember Picasso's Cubism from grade school art class, right? That abstract style with all the jumbled-up faces and mismatched angles? People say it was one of the greatest art movements of the

20th century. But to "kid me," it was just people broken into pieces and put back together kind of... weird.

Kind of like me—fractured, vivid, chaotic... and still holding together the whole picture somehow.

And yes, you are a work of art, too. But not the step-by-step, sip-wine-with-your-girlfriends kind of painting you do on a girls' night. You are a masterpiece. Some parts of you are obvious and loud. Some are quiet and hidden. Some are spicy and bold. Others are locked away behind rusty doors, waiting to be discovered. Some parts are quirky. Some, invisible.

But all of them are you. The one-of-a-kind original your kids call Mom.

The Morning It All Spilled Over

One morning, my husband and son were sitting at a red light at a large, bustling intersection. They were patiently waiting their turn when a jumbo garbage truck lumbered through the intersection and dropped a massive pile of trash right in the middle of the road. All the drivers stared in disbelief as the truck jerked forward, leaving behind a smoldering heap of debris. Then came the kicker—it wasn't just garbage. It was on fire.

And unfortunately, garbage sometimes does catch fire—like it did one morning in our own home, when my boys were very young. But this wasn't just any fire. It wasn't from a truck. It was my own emotional garbage fire, and it exploded all over the people I loved most.

It was a work morning, and I was trying to get everyone out the door and dropped off at school so I could make it to an important meeting. I rushed through the house, mentally juggling my task list, moving fast and trying to hold it all together. I was freshly showered, makeup on, dressed for work—and already sweating. My jaw was tight. My body was tense. The pressure was palpable.

Then the arguing started. Not over something important, of course. Just a normal sibling squabble about who would get the little green bowl for breakfast cereal. Colin (my youngest son) wanted it. Ryan wanted to play keep-away, big brother style. The cereal clinks felt deafening.

And I wish I could tell you I handled it with calm wisdom and expert-level parenting skills. I wish I could say I diffused the situation gracefully and with compassion. But that would be a lie.

The noise wasn't just around me—it was inside me, vibrating in my bones, like every cereal clink and whine was pressing a bruise I didn't know I had. And then—I snapped.

"Stop! Enough already! GIVE him the bowl!" I shouted, my voice sharp and rising. Ryan handed it over, but the storm had just begun. "Hurry up! Eat your breakfast! Get your backpack! Get in the car!"

Every word I spoke was like a match—soaked in stress, sparked by panic, and flung into a room full of kindling. They did what I said—teary-eyed and silent—but the damage was done.

Once they were finally buckled into the car, I kept going. Guilt trips. Disappointment. Shame. All of it came pouring out like hot ash. I dropped them off at school, drove to work, and somewhere along the way, the fire fizzled.

That's when the guilt kicked in.

Not the light kind that nudges you to do better—but the heavy, searing shame that comes when you realize you've turned your kids into collateral damage. The kind that sits in your chest and whispers, "You're the problem." I gripped the steering wheel and blinked hard, wishing I could turn the car around, scoop my kids up, and take it all back.

And maybe you're wondering, "Why didn't you just get up ear-lier?" Or "Why didn't you plan ahead?" Or even "Couldn't you just have been late?" And yes. Yes to all of it. I could have done a dozen things differently that morning. But I didn't.

Instead of taking my emotional trash out—processing it, releas-ing it—I let it build up. And on that day, it caught fire. I dumped it right on my kids. My load had gotten too heavy, too volatile. And instead of a gentle release, it became a full-blown blaze.

"You yelled. You slammed the door. You overreacted. And now shame whispers, 'You're the problem.' But shame is a liar. It keeps you stuck where repair wants to set you free." – Angel McKim

From Breakdown to Breakthrough

That's the moment I realized: I didn't need more discipline or better time management. I needed a different part of myself to step forward—the part that could manage the emotional load before it spilled onto everyone else.

I needed The Clean Sweep.

Because the truth is, emotions don't just disappear. When we don't make time to clear out what's building up inside—re-sentment, overwhelm, exhaustion—it piles up. And sometimes, what piles up isn't just today's frustration—it's years of holding it together, of being the calm one, the strong one, the one who never falls apart. Until one day, you do.

When our nervous system flips into fight or flight, the thinking part of the brain (the prefrontal cortex) temporarily goes offline.

Logic, patience, and empathy take a back seat to survival. That's not failure—it's biology.

"You wanna fly, you got to give up the sh– that weighs you down." – Toni Morrison

What Is The Clean Sweep, Really?

When we shout, our kids might obey—but they also absorb our overwhelm like sponges, carrying away silent questions about their worth. And while they may not say it out loud, they're wondering: Am I the reason mom is upset? Am I too much?

That's why learning how to do a clean sweep—before the fire—can change everything.

We all have those days when we just need a break—a chance to recharge, reset, and breathe. Debbie Phelps called them "Debbie Days," where once a month she'd take time for herself and do something she loved. And don't get me wrong—Debbie Days are wonderful and necessary. But a single day of rest can't undo the damage from a week of emotional smoke inhalation.

That's where the Clean Sweep comes in.

"No one ever taught me how to clear my own emotions. I just learned to carry them quietly." – Angel McKim

Before you can fill yourself up with all the good stuff—like rest, joy, connection—you have to make space. You have to clear out what's weighing you down.

Strengthening your Clean Sweep is a mental fitness muscle you must practice regularly to stay grounded, emotionally available, and mentally well. Because here's the thing: when we don't make time to process the hard stuff—resentment, exhaustion, stress—it piles up. And that pile gets heavy. Toxic. Flammable.

A once-a-month recharge won't cut it if you're dragging around an overflowing load of emotional garbage every day. You can't just be the garbage can for everyone else's stress. You have to become the one who clears it out.

The Clean Sweep isn't about perfection or polished routines. It's about making small, regular efforts to stay emotionally clear and mentally strong. You don't wait for the trash to overflow—you take it out, again and again, as often as needed.

Because why settle for one peaceful day a month... when you could make every day lighter?

Signs You're Due for a Sweep

As a mom of a child with ADHD, you're already hauling plenty. And I'm not just talking about empty snack wrappers or laundry baskets. I'm talking about the emotional weight of parenting a child who may wake up grumpy, argue over socks, push every limit, and resist bedtime like it's a personal attack.

Parenting any child can be demanding. Parenting a child with ADHD can feel like trying to tidy a house in a windstorm. You're dodging meltdowns, trying to stay calm, managing your own triggers—and doing it all while holding down a job, a household, and a sliver of a personal life.

That's a lot of emotional debris to manage. And if you're not intentional about clearing it, it will build up. This is why strengthening your Clean Sweep muscle is not just helpful—it's essential.

And it's why pausing—even briefly—can be the difference between surviving and breathing again.

"Almost everything will work again if you unplug it for a few minutes, including you." – Anne Lamott

This Is a Muscle—And You're Building It

The Clean Sweep isn't just about letting go of stress—it's about how we show up when the tension is high, and the pressure is on. It's often a dance between the fierce part of you—the one that holds the line and builds grit—and the tender part of you—the one that sees into your child's heart and makes them feel safe and deeply loved.

In my work coaching moms of kids with ADHD, I once partnered with a mom who embodied this very tension. She was ambitious, loving, and deeply committed to her kids. She had an incredibly tender side—one that brought calm and comfort to her son like no one else could. She was the soft landing place, especially in contrast to her husband, who brought more structure and firm authority.

But here's what we uncovered: her beautiful tenderness had become unbalanced. She was constantly pouring herself out, and in the process, becoming emotionally drained. Her days felt heavy. She was exhausted, overwhelmed, and far from the joyful, light-hearted mom she longed to be.

She did have a fierce side—but it only showed up when she hit her breaking point, when frustration boiled over into anger. And then, afterward, came the guilt.

What she really needed was a balanced fierce—the kind that sets boundaries, says "not right now," and protects her peace without guilt. She didn't need to be angry. She needed to be grounded.

That balance? It doesn't start with a schedule or a strategy. It starts inside you.

It starts when you notice you're feeling full—full of stress, frustration, pressure—and you take action to clear it out. You pause. You step away. You move your body. You breathe. You do what needs to be done to reset your nervous system. You make a Clean Sweep.

Because your kids are watching. They are learning how to handle stress by watching how you handle yours. They're learning when to be fierce and when to be tender by watching you model both.

Maybe your balance looks different from another mom's. Maybe you tend to lead with fierce and it creates more battles than connection. Or maybe you lead with tenderness and find yourself stretched thin, emotionally spent.

Either way—if you feel off balance, that's okay. This is a muscle—one you weren't taught to build, but one you're strong enough to grow. Every pause, every breath, every reset strengthens it.

Once you learn when to lead with fierceness and when to soften into tenderness—on purpose—you've strengthened your Clean Sweep muscle. And the more you practice it, the lighter your days feel, and the more resilient you become.

Fast Tools to Clear the Emotional Load

> *"We need to replace your vicious stress cycle with a vicious cycle of self-care." – Dr. Sara Gottfried*

Here are a few quick, research-backed ways to clear emotional overload—especially when the fire's about to spark.

Deep Breathing

A few slow, conscious breaths can deactivate your stress response and bring your body back to calm. Try box breathing: inhale for 4, hold for 4, exhale for 4, hold for 4. Repeat.

"Feelings come and go like clouds in a windy sky. Conscious breathing is my anchor." – Thich Nhat Hanh

Physical Movement

Do some squats, take a walk, stretch your arms overhead—any movement that increases your heart rate will reduce muscle tension and boost brain clarity.

Create a Calming Anchor

Choose a simple gesture (like touching your thumb to your index finger or placing your hand over your heart). Pair it with a calming phrase or memory so your body starts to associate it with peace.

Visualization (used by pro athletes like Michael Phelps, LeBron James, Tom Brady)

Imagine a place where you feel calm, powerful, and safe. Visit this place in your mind to settle your system before a challenging moment.

Mental fitness isn't a one-and-done deal—it's a daily practice. So experiment. Try these tools. Mix them up. Find what works for you and keep it simple. The more often you do your Clean Sweep, the more you clear space for joy, connection, and calm.

Are You the Garbage Can... or the Clean Sweep?

Every mom lands somewhere on this spectrum. Some carry it all. Some clear it out. And some hold it in until it erupts.

The Garbage Can

Carries everyone's mess and emotions until overflow.
- Success Means...Getting through the week without completely falling apart.

- When Failure Happens...Collapses under the weight of everyone's needs.

- What Kids Might Learn..."Mom's overwhelmed—so I'd better stay small."

The Clean Sweep

Notices when it's time to release and reset.
- Success Means...Staying emotionally light by clearing the load regularly.

- When Failure Happens...Pauses. Regroups. Tries again with grace.

- What Kids Might Learn..."Everyone has big feelings—and we can handle them together."

> **The Time Bomb**
>
> Stores stress, anger, and exhaustion until it explodes.
> - Success Means...Controlling everything and everyone—until it all breaks.
>
> - When Failure Happens...Melts down, lashes out, then drowns in guilt or blame.
>
> - What Kids Might Learn..."Big emotions are dangerous. I have to hide mine."

Here's What Matters Most

"True resilience isn't about never breaking—it's about finding your way back to peace, again and again." – Inspired by Dr. Rick Hanson

You don't have to be a perfect parent with a perfectly scheduled self-care routine. But you can be the kind of mom who notices when the emotional load is getting heavy, catches the sparks early, and takes action before everything ignites. That's the power of The Clean Sweep—pausing to clear space for your own emotional balance so there's more of you to give to the ones you love most.

You can't show up with love or clarity when you're overflowing. But when you care for your own well-being, you model emotional resilience—the kind your child will carry for life. Because the greatest gift you can give your child isn't just a calm home—it's a calm you.

"Maybe growth isn't about never losing it—it's about finding your way back faster, with more grace each time." – Unknown

Reflection:

Take a deep breath before you read on. These questions aren't for judgment—they're for grace.

- When was the last time you felt your "emotional garbage" starting to overflow?

- What helped you take out the trash—and what might help you next time?

You don't need to carry it all alone. Every time you choose to pause, breathe, and clear space for yourself, you're teaching your child something sacred: that love can be steady, even when life is not.

Part 3: Leading a Family That Thrives, Not Just Survives

The strongest families aren't built by fixing each other—but by growing together.

CHAPTER 8

Raising a Family That Grows Together

The storms of family life can feel endless. But inside every hard moment is a chance to steady the boat—and strengthen the bonds that keep you afloat.

You may have started this journey thinking it was about helping one child. The child with the big emotions, the constant motion, the impulsive outbursts. But somewhere along the way, maybe you realized: this isn't just about them.

It affects how mornings sound—the thud of forgotten shoes, the rush of "Where's my backpack?" echoing down the hall. It changes how dinner feels—the chatter, the interruptions, the sigh you let out when the fork clatters mid-story. It shapes how your other children tiptoe through tense moments, how you and your partner exchange that quiet look across the room that says, We're both hanging on.

It touches everything—the air, the pace, the pulse of your days. But here's the other side of that coin: healing is just as contagious. One small shift—a calmer tone, a slower breath, a softer glance—can ripple through a household faster than any meltdown ever did.

When one person begins to self-regulate, the atmosphere changes—like opening a window after a long storm. Voices lower. Shoulders drop. The air feels lighter. When you parent with intention instead of survival, the energy shifts from bracing to breathing. Your calm becomes theirs. Your steadiness, their safety. That's how healing spreads—one quiet nervous system at a time.

"People will forget what you said, people will forget what you did, but people will never forget how you made them feel." – Maya Angelou

Part 3 of this book is about that shift—the slow, steady transformation that happens when you stop trying to control every storm and start learning how to steady the boat instead. It's about trading survival for connection, pressure for presence, and fear for trust.

Because this journey was never just about fixing one child—it's about building a family that can breathe, bend, and grow together.

But before that kind of growth begins, many families—maybe yours, too—start in a very different place: the fix-it zone.

When Fixing Becomes the Family Default

When you're deep in "I have to fix my kid" mode, it's wild how quickly your entire family dynamic starts to shift. Maybe you know that feeling—the constant scanning for what might go wrong next, the mental tabs always open, the tension that hums in your chest before anyone's even said a word.

I remember working with a mom whose son began struggling in early elementary school. At first, it was no big deal. Just a few tough days here and there. A "wait and see" kind of season. But then things snowballed.

His grades began to slip and the school's number lit up her phone again and again until she flinched at the sound. Homework battles stretched into long, tear-streaked nights—the house echoing with slammed doors and deep sighs—and that early curiosity hardened into a tight, panicked knot she carried in her chest.

Her husband was working long hours, so she became the default responder—fielding teacher emails, scouring parenting forums at midnight, trying to find something, anything, that would help. And when nothing worked? The "loud discussions" began.

"No, that is not okay!" she snapped one night, exhausted.

"What do you mean?" her husband asked.

"The teacher! She should be helping him more—making sure he understands. We can't do all the teaching for her," she said with exasperation.

"I think it's more than just the teacher," he said quietly.

They argued about all the usual suspects: medication, supplements, behavior, discipline, screen time, sugar. What to try. What to say. Who was doing too much—or not enough. And somewhere in all of it... she forgot.

In the chaos of trying to fix things, she forgot that her other child needed her too—needed time, tenderness, and a steady place to land. And I wish I could say that's when they called me. Those things turned around right then and there. But that's not how it went.

They kept spinning, faster and faster—like a carousel they couldn't step off. The stress wrapped around them, tighter each day, until even laughter sounded brittle. Threads of connection started to snap in small, silent ways, and a heavy fog of hopelessness settled over the house. Meals grew quieter. Bedtimes stretched longer. Even laughter—their old lifeline—felt forced, like they were all pretending not to drown.

That was the breaking point.

"Vulnerability is not winning or losing; it's having the courage to show up and be seen when you have no control over the outcome." – Brené Brown

It was the moment they realized something had to shift. Not just with their son. With the system. Because when one part of the family is struggling, the ripple touches everyone.

And nowhere is that ripple more visible than between siblings...

When One Child Fills the Whole Room

"Family life isn't about avoiding the chaos—it's about learning how to hold each other steady inside it." – Unknown

It's not on purpose. It's not neglect. It's not because you love your other children any less. It's just that sometimes, when one child needs more, the rest of the house exhales. Conversations lower to whispers. Laughter thins out. The air feels heavy with everything unsaid.

If you're parenting a child with ADHD, chances are they take up more space in your day—more energy, more conversations, more intervention. That's not a judgment. It's reality. And for their sibling? That dynamic can feel like growing up in someone else's shadow.

They may learn to go along, to be "easy," to not cause more trouble. They may keep their emotions tidy because there's no room for extra noise. Or maybe they go the other way—acting out in a bid to get attention that doesn't feel freely given anymore. Neither response is wrong. It's just their way of coping. They're just trying to find oxygen in a house where one child's needs sometimes fill every corner. They're figuring out how to matter without making more noise.

One mom I worked with described her daughter as "the steady one." Quiet, reliable, helpful. But over time, her daughter began snapping at her brother, withdrawing from family time, and making sharp little comments about "how everything's always about him." And you know what? She wasn't wrong.

When a child has ADHD, it's easy to become hyper-focused on their progress, their triggers, their potential blow-ups. So easy, in fact, that you stop seeing the other child's quiet signals. Let's be real—if you've got more than one kid, nobody's sitting this out. Everyone gets pulled into the swirl.

While one child is getting the spotlight, the other is watching and absorbing. They're learning patience, resilience, emotional flexibility—whether they signed up for it or not. But they're also learning where they fit in the family. And if we're not intentional, they can start to believe that love and attention only show up in times of struggle.

That's why part of parenting a child with ADHD is slowing down long enough to really see their siblings—the way their shoulders tense when chaos erupts, the small sigh when they think no one's watching. Validation isn't a grand speech; it's the quiet glance that says, I see you too.

It doesn't have to be a big overhaul. It can start with small, simple moments:

- Calling out a strength you've noticed that's not related to how "easy" they are

- Taking five minutes to do something that's just for the two of you

- Letting them express frustration without shutting it down or asking them to "be the bigger person"

- Reminding them that their emotions matter just as much as anyone else's

Because in a home where one child often needs more, the other child still needs to be seen. They don't need everything to be even. But they do need to know they matter. And when they know that? They don't just cope. They thrive.

"Fair doesn't mean everyone gets the same. Fair means everyone gets what they need." – Rick Riordan

The Pulse of the House: Your Partnership Sets the Rhythm

"Happy partnerships aren't built on perfect love—they're sustained by friendship." – Adapted from Friedrich Nietzsche

If your family were a body, your partnership would be the heartbeat. Steady or stressed, quiet or tense—it sets the rhythm for everything else. That doesn't mean you and your partner have to be perfectly aligned at all times (has anyone ever managed that?). But it does mean your relationship—how you speak to each other, how you handle stress, how you navigate decisions—shapes the emotional tone your kids live inside. They're watching. They're listening. They're learning what love sounds like under pressure.

When one parent is all-in on ADHD strategies and the other is skeptical or avoidant, it creates confusion—not just between the two of you, but for your child. They feel it when you're not on the same page. And while it's okay to have different personalities and parenting styles, what matters most is how you repair, reconnect, and realign when things go off track.

One mom I worked with shared how every parenting disagreement with her husband started to feel like a personal failure. She wanted connection. He wanted structure. She read the books. He scrolled news articles. The result? A low hum of resentment that followed them from dinner to bedtime. And guess who picked up on it? Their son.

It wasn't until they sat down together—not to argue, but to listen—that things started to shift. Not with all the answers—just with honesty and heart. You don't need a flawless partnership to shape a strong family—you just need to show up with intention and a willingness to grow together. And that starts with pausing long enough to ask each other:

- What kind of environment do we want our kids to grow up in?

- What do we each need to feel supported right now?

- How can we model teamwork, even when we disagree?

It's not about being in sync all the time—it's about learning how to reconnect when you fall out of step.

Your child's regulation is tethered to your own heartbeat—and beneath that, to the weather inside your walls. Your partnership is the barometer. When tension builds, everyone feels the pressure drop. When you soften, the air clears, and warmth drifts back in.

Storms will come—the kind that rattle the windows and soak you to the bone. But the sunlight always returns, spilling warmth across the same floors that once held tears. Every day, you get to choose the weather inside your home—to open the curtains, to let the light back in, to help your family grow toward it. And that same principle applies beyond your partnership—to the way you lead, teach, and show up for your children.

Because family life isn't just about managing the storms—it's about modeling how to move through them.

From Managing to Modeling: The Shift That Changes Everything

If you're anything like most moms raising a child with ADHD, you've probably asked yourself...

- How do I get them to listen?

- How do I get them to stop melting down?

- How do I get them to care about school, chores, other people?

All natural questions—especially when you're in the thick of stress. But the longer you're on this parenting path, the more those questions starts to evolve. It shifts from "How do I get them to...?" to "What do I want them to learn from me?" Because here's the truth: you're not just managing behavior. You're modeling how to be in the world. How to handle frustration without exploding. How to own a mistake and make it right. How to stay curious during conflict. How to honor your values, even when things feel messy.

This doesn't mean you have to be calm and composed all the time. It just means you're willing to notice your impact, come back to connection, and keep growing forward—together. That's what thriving families do. They don't avoid struggle—they work through it. They don't aim for perfection—they return to repair. Because that willingness—to keep showing up with heart—changes everything.

Maybe it's sitting down once a week to check in as a family. Maybe it's taking a pause before reacting to a meltdown. Maybe it's naming your family values out loud—and using them to guide decisions big and small.

These aren't grand gestures. They're daily rhythms. And over time, they create the kind of steady, safe foundation that helps every member of your family thrive.

Not perfectly. But on purpose.

Simple Tools to Help Your Family Thrive

You don't need fancy systems or a perfectly choreographed household to build a thriving family. What you need are simple, meaningful ways to stay grounded, stay connected, and grow on purpose. These tools are here to help you do just that. These tools can be downloaded for free at happyrevolutions.com/myfamily.

Family Core Values Worksheet

Get clear on what matters most. This worksheet helps you identify 3–5 guiding values for your family—so everyone knows what you stand for and how to return to those anchors when things get hard.

Create a Family Mission Statement

This is about more than cute wall art. When your family has a clear "why," it becomes easier to make decisions, set boundaries, and move through tough moments with shared purpose.

Here's What Matters Most

You're not just raising a child with ADHD. You're raising a family.

And that means what you model—especially in the messy, imperfect moments—shapes how everyone grows. Your steadiness teaches resilience. Your repair teaches trust. Your willingness to keep showing up—even when you're tired, uncertain, or stretched thin—plants something deep and lasting.

You don't need a perfect routine or an ideal response for every hard moment. What your family really needs is you—present, learning, leading with heart.

"What you do every day matters more than what you do once in a while." – Gretchen Rubin

When one person begins to heal, the whole family shifts. Little by little, chaos gives way to calm, and you realize: you're building something beautiful. Not flawless—just intentional.

Keep modeling what matters. Keep choosing connection. Because one day, you'll look back and see it—the mornings softer, the home lighter, the family steady in its rhythm again.

"Out of difficulties grow miracles." – Jean de La Bruyère

As your family learns to bend, breathe, and grow together, something else begins to happen—quietly, almost without notice. The focus starts to shift inward. Because the truth is, family healing always begins with the one who decides to look within.

And that person... is you.

CHAPTER 9

You Are the Pivot Point

Different Roots, Same Heart

Parenting isn't just what we do. It's what we pass on. Every family carries echoes of the one that came before it. If you've ever caught yourself reacting like your parents and thought, "Wait—where did that come from?" you're not alone. It's not failure. It's wiring, and awareness is the first rewrite...

I was chatting with a mom about the differences between Baby Boomers, Gen X and Millennials. We were laughing and joking about parenthood and how different our own childhoods were from our kids.

"Let's face it," she laughed. "Almost everything we know about parenthood, we learned from our parents."

"Oh God" I said as I shot her a concerned smile. "I am not my mother." I reaffirmed.

"Well, who do you think taught you your parenting skills? Our kids didn't come with instruction manuals—but that would have been nice!"

"Ha!" I beamed her a smile.

But she was right. I hadn't magically learned how to be a "mom", I had acquired much of my parenting style from my parents. Maybe I picked up some new ideas, tips, and tricks from those wonderful parenting books I've read, but for the most part, when times get tough, I revert right back to the familiar.

"You know?", she paused as her eyes shifted to the ceiling.

"We definitely grew up in times where 'tough love' was the prevailing parenting style.

I laughed out loud, almost spitting my drink all over myself. "Yeah, if you can call that a 'parenting style.'"

I continued. "I can still hear my moms voice in my head with her finger wagging in my face and yelling 'go to your room.'"

"Yeah, me too." she sighed. "I was sent to my room too...a lot. To 'deal with it', 'shake it off', or 'figure it out' on my own." She cracked a funny-not-funny smile as we continued to reminisce about our childhoods.

"Yup" she said. "There was definitely zero tolerance for screw-ups at my house and my dad definitely saw crying as a sign of weakness—especially from my brothers"

I half laughed as I drifted back to my own childhood memories.

The more I thought about her comments the more I realized it's what so many of us have in common.

Maybe we grew up with different family structures and relationships—maybe we lived in different communities and went to different types of schools; but our mistakes were the same. Our mistakes, big and small, were often not treated as learning opportunities for growth—they were moments to feel small, ashamed, or afraid.

> *"We repeat what we don't repair." – Christine Langley-Obaugh*

When Good Isn't Good Enough

There's a moment that lives quietly in so many of us—the sting of getting something wrong and feeling the air shift. A teacher's sigh. A parent's disappointment. The look that says, "You should've known better.

> *"Breaking a cycle doesn't mean you hate where you came from. It means you love where you're going." – Unknown*

Unfortunately, generations of the past simply didn't have the necessary tools and skills to help us navigate our big mistakes. Instead of having emotionally open and honest conversations about struggle, mistakes, and "big feelings", we were often left to create our own "coping strategies" (good and bad).

Maybe you learned early that mistakes carried shame—that being "good" meant keeping your voice small and your hands folded. And that being "strong" meant swallowing tears before anyone could see them. And before you knew it, you carried those same expectations into adulthood.

Now, as a grown woman, you're still chasing that invisible gold star—stretching a little higher for approval that never quite lands, whispering, "What was I thinking?" Those whispers don't stay inside your head. They leak into your parenting—especially on the hardest days.

And if you look closer, you'll see it: That same patterns show up when your child is still struggling, when progress feels out of reach, and when you're too tired to keep pretending you've got it all together.

In the quiet after bedtime, when the house finally exhales, you stand in the hallway, whispering, "Am I really the right mom for this?" That question doesn't make you weak. It makes you *awake*.

"Hard days aren't proof you're broken. They're proof that you're doing the work your parents never got to do." – Unknown

Of course, not everyone grew up in a "tough love" household. Maybe your parents were gentle and emotionally present. Maybe one was nurturing while the other struggled in ways they didn't even recognize. Maybe your home was full of love—but light on tools.

Whatever your story, here's what I've seen again and again: Every mom raising a child with ADHD eventually gets invited to look inward.

Sometimes that invitation shows up as perfectionism. Sometimes it's people-pleasing. Sometimes it's fear, control, or the nagging sense of never being enough. Still, the invitation asks the same question: Do you want to grow through this—or just get through it?

Pause and breathe. That voice of exhaustion carries generations of mothers doing the best they could. You're just the first to stop and choose differently.

Now ask yourself:

- How do I treat myself when I make a mistake?

- Does your child see you offer yourself compassion?

- Get curious about what went wrong?

- Or do they see you spiral into those same old emotions—anger, guilt, shame?

Because here's what I know about you. You want to raise a child who can breathe easy in their own skin—open-hearted, light-shouldered, unshaken by every stumble. The fact that you're here—reading these words in the middle of another busy day, coffee gone cold, laundry waiting, heart still tender from yesterday's chaos—means something.

You are the bridge between what was and what will be, standing barefoot in the middle of it all, whispering, "This stops with me."

You're not doing it alone, Mama. There's a whole chorus of us walking that same bridge beside you.

You've already started the change just by noticing. Even on the days it feels invisible, growth is happening beneath the surface. Every moment you choose awareness over autopilot, you're fueling something bigger—a quiet revolution of love.

That quiet revolution doesn't always start with grand gestures—it starts right here, in the mess of everyday moments. When you take a deep breath instead of raising your voice. When you whisper "It's okay" after spilling the milk. When you circle back after a hard moment and say, "I'm sorry."

Each one of those moments is a seed of healing—tiny, ordinary acts that slowly rewrite your family's story.

The Quiet Revolution

In every ordinary moment—over coffee cups and crayons, over sighs and second chances—every choice you make plants a seed of hope and change in your family's story. And over time, those seeds take root—stretching toward the light, cracking old patterns open until something new begins to bloom: a quiet revolution. A happy revolution. One where healing hums through kitchen tables and bedtime stories. Where families grow—not perfectly, but powerfully—together. That idea shaped my mission—and became Happy Revolutions, a quiet, brave, everyday calling to help families grow together.

And here's what I've learned after walking beside so many moms of kids with ADHD: You're going to spill the milk. Raise your voice. Slam a door. Say something you wish you could take back. Yet when your child sees you fall apart—and then pick yourself back up—they learn something way more important. They learn resilience. They learn grace. They learn what it means to be human.

And for a child with ADHD, who's often told they're "too much" or "not enough," that lesson is *everything*. What you want more than anything is to help your child turn their struggles into strengths—to help them build the real, lasting skills that lead to happiness and success. That's why I believe the best way to help our kids become happy, successful adults—is to partner with them and grow right alongside them.

Let's be real—parenting is hard. Parenting a child with ADHD? That's a full-contact sport. But learning to do it well can become the most magical, meaningful journey of your life. And that story you're building? It won't be built on perfection. It will be built on healing. On doing the work your parents may not have known how to do. On showing up anyway.

What we're building here, Mama, isn't just a calmer day or a softer morning. It's a story stitched together in small moments—the laughter after tears, the hug after a hard day, the steady hand that reaches back for theirs.

"Parenthood... It's about guiding the next generation, and forgiving the last." – Peter Krause

Every seed you plant in love has roots that reach backward—into every story, voice, and lesson you came from. This is what cycle-breakers do. They grow forward with both hands open—one holding what was, the other building what's next. It's not loud or perfect. It's love in motion.

And it's how we build families that thrive, one quiet revolution at a time.

The Legacy You're Building Now

We all carry patterns from the past. Some are beautiful. Some are painful. Some we swore we'd never repeat—but still find ourselves reenacting on the hardest days. When you choose to parent differently, you're not just helping your child thrive in the now. You're rewriting what gets passed on next. This is the power you hold right now—the power to pivot from what was into what can be.

"You can't go back and change the beginning, but you can start where you are and change the ending." – C.S. Lewis

Here's what you can choose to pass on.

Emotional Safety

You're showing your child that their feelings aren't "too much." That their tears don't scare you. That even in the heat of a meltdown, they are still safe, still loved, still yours. That's not coddling—it's connection. It's giving them the emotional foundation you may never got to stand on yourself.

Self-Awareness

You're helping your child notice what's happening inside their body—the tight chest, the fast breath, the storm behind their eyes—and name it before it takes over. You're modeling what it looks like to pause, to say, "I'm feeling overwhelmed right now. I'm going to take a breath." That kind of language becomes a lifelong compass—one that points them back to calm again and again.

Open Communication

You're showing your kids that hard conversations don't break love. That they can come to you with the messy, the confusing, the unfinished. That they don't have to hide, perform, or pretend. Even if you weren't raised in a home where feelings were spoken out loud—you're building one now.

Resilience

You're teaching your child how to rise again. Not by forcing strength, but by lending your steadiness. By standing beside them in the hard moments and saying, "I'm not going anywhere." That's what builds grit—not the absence of struggle, but the presence of someone who stays.

Self-Trust

When your child sees you choosing growth over guilt—pausing instead of snapping, repairing instead of retreating—they begin to trust that mistakes aren't the end of the story. They learn that it's safe to try again, to fail, to be seen. And that's how self-trust takes root—quietly, deeply, in the soil of your everyday moments.

You may not have grown up with all of this. But you can choose it now—through your words, your patience, your presence. And that choice? That's how cycles break. That's how healing begins to echo forward.

Small Steps, Big Legacy

This is where insight becomes action—the small, repeatable steps that make change stick on real-life Tuesdays when everyone's melting down. You don't have to fix everything by Friday. Legacy isn't built in sweeping changes—it's grown through quiet, intentional choices repeated in the rhythm of real life.

These tools are here to help you reflect, reset, and keep growing:

Generational Patterns Reflection

Sometimes the first step forward is simply seeing what's already here. Take a moment to gently name what's been passed down to you—not to blame, but to understand. Ask yourself:

- What did love look like in your family growing up?

- How was conflict handled?

- What emotions were welcomed—and which ones were not?

- What did you learn about failure?

- About success?

- About being "good"?

Now ask: Which of those patterns are you carrying forward—and which ones are you ready to lay down?

"What I Want to Pass On" Letter

Here's a heart-centered way to anchor what matters most. Write a short letter to your child (or your future self as a parent). In it, name what you hope your child remembers about their childhood—what you want them to feel, believe, and know deep in their bones.

You don't have to give it to them. Just writing it brings clarity—and reminds you what's worth protecting in the noise of everyday life.

Power Trait Strength Check-In

Growth isn't about mastering every skill—it's about noticing which ones are blooming and which ones need more light. Look back at the Power Traits in this book.

Ask yourself:

- Where am I strongest right now?

- Which ones still feel like a stretch?

- What's one Power Trait I want to grow into more fully in this next season?

- How can I practice it in small, sustainable ways?

Remember: You're not behind. You're just building your own version of strength—one practice at a time.

Start a Legacy List: 10 Small Choices with a Big Impact

Legacy isn't a grand plan—it's a collection of everyday choices that whisper, this is who we are.

You don't need a five-year plan to make a legacy-level impact.

Start with ten tiny shifts that move you and your family toward connection, trust, and resilience. Here are a few ideas to get you going:

I'll pause before reacting.

I'll repair after a hard moment.

I'll tell my child what I love about them—unprompted.

I'll speak gently, even when I set firm boundaries.

I'll tell the truth about how I'm feeling.

I'll ask for help when I need it.

I'll let my child see me trying again after I mess up.

I'll apologize when I get it wrong.

I'll rest without guilt.

I'll keep showing up—even when it's hard.

Legacy isn't built in one moment—it's shaped by the choices we repeat when no one's watching, and felt by the ones who call us mom. These small steps might not look dramatic on paper—but they change everything in real life. Because what you practice quietly today becomes the legacy your family will feel tomorrow.

Here's What Matters Most

Every hard conversation you stay present for. Every gentle repair after a tough moment. Every time you model honesty, self-compassion, or courage—you're rewriting the story. Most of us weren't handed a playbook filled with emotional fluency or calm conflict resolution. Many of us were handed perfectionism. Silence. Shame. A model that said, Do better—but don't feel too much. But you? You're doing it differently. Not perfectly—but on purpose.

That difference? It ripples. Through your children. Through your home. Through generations you'll never meet. You don't need to become a new person. You just need to become more of the person you're already trying to be—more aware, more anchored, more open to growth.

Legacy doesn't come from having all the answers. It comes from the willingness to keep asking better questions. To look back with clarity and forward with love. The work you're doing—this quiet, everyday work—matters more than you know.

So keep going. Keep showing up. What you model today will echo for years—in their voices, in their choices, in the way they love, and in the quiet ways they'll one day steady someone else, just like you did. And one day, long after the noise and homework battles fade, when your child reaches for their own little one and whispers the same soft words you once did, you'll realize the shift wasn't loud or sudden—it was woven through love that learned to listen.

You'll know: This is it. This is the legacy you've built.

*"I thought I was teaching my child how to be resilient.
But really, they've been teaching me." – Reader comment*

Chapter 10

This Is Just the Beginning

This isn't a book about fixing your child. It's a book about becoming the parent your child already believes you are.

"What we know matters, but who we are matters more."
– Brené Brown

Maybe you thought that by now you'd have this figured out. Maybe you thought you'd be calmer, more consistent, more confident. That you'd yell less. That your routines would run smoother. That your child would have "made more progress." But here's the truth most people don't say out loud: growth rarely looks like a straight line. It unfolds in quiet moments, subtle shifts, and second chances.

So if you're still hitting rough mornings or bedtime meltdowns or days where you wonder if anything you're doing is working—you're not failing. You're human. You're learning. You're showing up. Because the real work isn't about becoming the "perfect parent." It's about being the safe place your child can come back to—even after hard moments. Especially after hard moments.

You're not behind. You're not too late. You're right on time. And everything you've done—every effort, every repair, every time you came back with a softer tone or steadier heart—is already changing things.

"Do the best you can until you know better. Then when you know better, do better." – *Maya Angelou*

Thriving Is a Long Game

It's tempting to measure progress in milestones. The good week at school. The meltdown-free dinner. The morning that didn't end in tears (yours or theirs). Those moments feel like finish lines.

But thriving? Thriving doesn't look like a single win. It looks like movement over time.

It looks like fewer blowups, and quicker repairs. Like a little more laughter, a little more calm. Like being able to say, "That was hard," and still stay connected. Like knowing your child better—what sets them off, what helps them settle, what lights them up.

Thriving isn't about getting to the point where nothing ever goes wrong. It's about having the tools, the language, and the self-trust to find your way through when things do go wrong. Because here's the truth: ADHD parenting doesn't follow a traditional timeline. Some of the changes you're working toward—better emotional regulation, stronger self-awareness, deeper connection—don't always show up in test scores or behavior charts.

They show up in tiny moments:

- When your child calms down just a little faster than they used to.

- When they apologize without being prompted.

- When you handle a tough moment with more grace than you had a year ago.

They show up in the long game.

And that's why you're here. Not to win the short game, but to build something strong enough to last. Something your child can stand on. Something you can be proud of—not because it's perfect, but because it's real.

> *"When we are no longer able to change a situation, we are challenged to change ourselves." – Viktor E. Frankl*

A Final Note

This isn't the end of the road. It's the beginning of a new way of walking it.

Because parenting a child with ADHD isn't just about managing behaviors—it's about becoming someone new in the process. Someone who listens more closely. Leads with heart. Models what it means to feel big things and still move forward.

> *"Children need love, especially when they do not deserve it." – Fred Rogers*

There will be days that stretch you. Days that knock the wind out of you. But there will also be moments—quiet, surprising moments—when you see your child growing into themselves...and realize you are, too. You don't have to know all the answers. You don't need to do it perfectly. You just have to keep showing up with curiosity, compassion, and the courage to try again.

You're not alone in this. You never were. And you don't have to do it alone anymore.

"There's no way to be a perfect mother and a million ways to be a good one."— Jill Churchill

Want to Keep Going?

If this book gave you a new lens or a little lift, I'd love to keep walking with you. Because you're doing the hardest work there is—and you deserve support that's just as strong.

Need help with the day-to-day?

From morning routines to homework battles to big feelings—I've created simple tools to make your daily life easier. Printable guides, mini courses, and real-life solutions designed for moms like you. You can explore them all at happyrevolutions.com.

Want a safe place to land?

Join a private Facebook community of moms raising kids with ADHD—where you can share stories, ask hard questions, and feel a little less alone.

Ready for real change at home?

Coaching is where we take everything you've learned here and turn it into transformation. Step-by-step, side-by-side. When you're ready, I'll be here.

Need a weekly boost?

Sign up for short & sweet encouragement in your in-box—bite-sized wisdom, practical tools, and reminders that you're not alone in this.

Loved the book?

Pass it on. If this helped you, it might help someone else too. We're better when we grow together.

Acknowledgements

To the mothers who keep showing up—with love, persistence, and an unshakable belief in their children—you are the heart of this book. Your courage and hope light the way for so many others.

To the families I've had the privilege to coach—thank you for your openness, your trust, and the lessons you've shared along the way. Your stories continue to shape and inspire my work.

And to the educators, clinicians, and advocates who pour their hearts into helping children with ADHD thrive—your dedication and support are changing the lives of generations.

Some of the voices that shaped this work are listed on the next page.

Books That Shaped This Work

This book was shaped by many things—my sons, my family, the moms I've coached, and the quiet moments where I realized something had to change.

The books listed here are the ones I directly reference in these pages. They helped shift my perspective, challenged old assumptions, and gave language to ideas I was already beginning to feel in my bones. They are not required reading. You don't need to read them all—or any of them—for this work to matter.

And just as important: these are not the only resources that shaped my thinking. This work has been influenced by years of reading, training, coaching, and walking alongside families like yours. Growth is living and evolving—and so is the learning that supports it.

Seeing ADHD Differently (and Finally Exhaling)

These books helped me stop trying to "fix" my child and start seeing ADHD through a strengths-based, human lens.

Normal Sucks — Jonathan Mooney

Life to the Extreme — Ty Pennington

Helping Kids (and Moms) Talk to Themselves with Kindness

These books shaped how I think about self-talk, emotional regulation, resilience, and mental fitness—for kids and parents alike.

Chatter: The Voice in Our Head, Why It Matters, and How to Harness It — Ethan Kross

Authentic Happiness / Flourish — Martin Seligman

Raising Kids for the Long Game (Not Just the Next Meltdown)

These books influenced how I think about parenting as leadership—rooted in patience, structure, belief, and steady support over time.

A Mother for All Seasons — Debbie Phelps

The Golden Rules — Bob Bowman

Believing in Your Child When the World Doesn't

These books helped shape my understanding of courage, identity, and what it means to stand beside a child who doesn't fit the mold—and to believe anyway.

Mum's the Word — Eve Branson

Like a Virgin — Richard Branson

The Virgin Way — Richard Branson

Staying Connected When Emotions Run High

This book shaped how I think about conflict, communication, and connection—especially when emotions are loud and the stakes feel high.

Never Split the Difference — Chris Voss

If you're curious about additional resources I recommend beyond this list, I share them regularly through my emails and community. Because learning doesn't end when the last page does—and neither does your growth.

You're not behind.

You're building something real.

And this really is just the beginning.

Ways to Stay Connected

If this book resonated with you, I want you to know this:

You don't have to do this alone.

Parenting a child with ADHD can feel isolating—especially when you're doing the inner work alongside the daily realities of emotions, school, and routines. Support isn't a sign that you're struggling. It's a sign that you *care*.

Facebook Group

A private online group for moms raising kids with ADHD—built on honesty, compassion, and real life. A place to share, ask questions, and feel understood. www.facebook.com/groups/adhdkidsambitiousmoms

Practical Tools

Simple, practical tools for real moments—morning routines, big emotions, homework battles, and more. Designed to make everyday life feel a little calmer.

happyrevolutions.com or angelmckim.com

Email

Just reach out and say hello. I promise I read every single email. angel@happyrevolutions.com

One Last Thing

You don't have to use every tool or strategy. You don't have to change all at once.

Take what helps. Leave what doesn't.

But let's connect. We grow better together.